S0-AVJ-864

Beyond Promises

Beyond Promises

A Biblical Challenge
to Promise Keepers

David Hagopian
Douglas Wilson

MOSCOW, IDAHO

© 1996, Canon Press, P.O. Box 8741, Moscow, ID 83843.

Published by Canon Press, 1996.

Cover design by Paige Atwood Design, Moscow, ID
Printed in the United States of America.

99 98 97 96   9 8 7 6 5 4 3 2 1

No part of this publication may be reproduced, stored in a retrieval system, or transmitted in any form by any means, electronic, mechanical, photocopy, recording, or otherwise, without prior permission of the publisher, except for brief quotations in critical reviews or articles.

Scripture references are taken from the New American Standard Bible, King James Version and New King James Version of the Bible.

ISBN: 1-885767-12-9

Beyond Promises
A Biblical Challenge to Promise Keepers

PART FOUR: BEYOND PROMISES

Foreword

John H. Armstrong

If the burgeoning movement known as "Promise Keepers" promises anything, it openly professes to stand for the Gospel of Jesus Christ in an increasingly secular age. It calls men to serve God, and to do so in the name of Jesus Christ. As this movement continues to grow, now hoping to reach a million men in this year, it is by the Gospel of Jesus Christ that it must be examined by those who are its true friends. Its size and ability to make an impact upon American males must not be the criterion for serious Christian analysis.

Critics have already lined up in strong opposition to Promise Keepers. Some are purely secular and their analyses are unchristian and decidedly secular. Others attempt to be Christian but sound so strident. Others have raised good questions. Most have been virtually drowned out by the positive impact made during the early stages of this vast new evangelical cause. After all, who can argue with the outward fruit of such a massive effort when husbands come home from conferences openly loving their wives in new ways, serving their families with renewed interest (some for the first time?), and honoring God in their churches in ways never before imagined?

In a land parched for spiritual reality, and in churches where expectations for recovery run quite high, it should not surprise us that evangelical Christianity has again birthed a growing movement from outside the church. (This has been our pattern, especially during this century.) What is surprising is how fast this particular movement has grown and how many pastors from such diverse backgrounds are now faced with the highly charged and complex question, "What will I do regarding the Promise Keepers movement?" (Over 40,000 pastors came to Atlanta in February, 1996, to consider their response to this new "move of God.")

Until this point much of the criticism of this movement has centered around issues that are often important but not always crucial. Concerns have been expressed regarding the lack of strong doctrinal teaching, the proliferation of charismatic leadership and worship styles (emotional excitement is often equated with the presence of God), the overuse of psychotherapeutic helping models, and the increasingly ecumenical nature of both the meetings and the leadership of the movement. In my own view, and in light of the direction of evangelical religion in this country generally, all of these are areas for genuine concern. But none of these concerns touch the real heart of the matter. In the end Promise Keepers is simply what evangelicalism has become, a movement without a doctrinally defined focus, that can draw multitudes to exciting events but without a theology of the church that will build Christ's church in a New Testament sense.

Any movement that claims so strongly and self-consciously to be grounded upon the revealed truths of the Gospel of Jesus Christ must be measured by the Gospel it professes allegiance to. This surely is not to ask too much. We are prone to judge things by numbers, excitement, impressive and engaging speakers, an ability to gain the attention of multitudes, even the testimonies of changed lives themselves. The proper means for judging anything which professes to be rooted in the Gospel is *by* the Gospel itself. The problem for the Promise Keepers movement is exactly what it is for much of modern evangelicalism—it simply has an inadequate view of the Gospel. This movement promises (no pun intended) so much, but unless it gains a proper understanding of the Gospel, it will ultimately give us what several generations of similar "revival" movements have already given us—emotional burn-out and doctrinal confusion and indifference. What is perhaps even worse is that we will have more spiritual casualties for the next generation.

To analyze anything that is broadly evangelical and remotely successful is not considered safe or wise. The authors of this book have shown wisdom in their approach to this highly-charged issue. Their choice of words is careful, their tone irenic in spirit, and their conclusions compelling if examined by the doctrine of *sola Scriptura* (Scripture as final authority for all matters of faith and practice). The product of their careful research and study is a readable, important, and necessary book.

One might argue that Christian writers should stick to positive writing and not critique contemporary movements. Some even take the approach of Gamaliel (Acts 5:34-40) suggesting we should never critique anything in the present time but allow God to show if it is from Him or from man. This is to confuse the counsel of an unbeliever with the more biblical counsel given to pastors to properly expose error as well as teach what is truth (*cf.* 1 & 2 Timothy).

I would hope that leaders of the Promise Keepers movement might consider the reasonable concerns and significant issues raised by Douglas Wilson and David Hagopian. I can hope for this, even though there is little evidence at present that this kind of openness exists. I pray, furthermore, that multitudes of men who are genuinely excited about the Promise Keepers movement will ponder the sober and biblical warnings of this fine book. You cannot go wrong if your confidence is truly grounded in Christ alone and in His written Word alone. Whatever else you may say about this book, you will be compelled by careful reading to admit that the writers have done their careful work and stated their concerns in a clear way.

I hope, finally, that pastors who are being pressured to "sign-on" with this movement will think about the important matters raised by a helpful book such as this. If you have been through several decades of evangelical life in America you must be somewhat weary of another "new move of God." This all sounds like previous "moves" except the excitement level is higher than ever. Are you not the least bit skeptical (in an honest and biblical sense) that something more profound is amiss than most of us may have imagined? You might even be asking, "What is the answer to the desperate need in my own church?" By God's grace you might find out that the power of God is in a message, not in a technique, or a massive movement. In the process you just might be transformed by the power of that message and begin to preach it with God-given power. If you decide to make the Gospel the chief concern of your labor for Christ, you will be both honored and hated. The whole effort will be worth the trials if you will but remember that you will give account to the Chief Shepherd in the Last Day. You must do only two things to be a faithful pastor and neither requires you to sign on to the movements of our age. The Apostle counsels you, my fellow minister, to

> Watch your life and doctrine closely. Persevere in them, because if you do you will save both yourself and your hearers (1 Tim. 4:16).

Acknowledgments

We want to thank Sam Pepke for asking the right questions that led to the birth of this project, Rod Randall for emphasizing the positive impact of the movement, Jeffery Sikkema for his valuable time, Bill Baldwin for his keen theological insights, and the families of Redeeming Grace Presbyterian Church in Laguna Hills, California and Community Evangelical Fellowship in Moscow, Idaho for their support and encouragement. We also want to thank whoever it was that invented the Internet, making long distance book cooperation a reasonable undertaking.

We thank our wives, Jamie Hagopian and Nancy Wilson, for their editorial mastery, and for the support they give in countless ways, some of which we see and understand.

We thank Promise Keepers for providing press credentials for the Dallas 1995 conference, and Strang Communications for the complimentary copies of *New Man* magazine.

John Armstrong was kind enough to write the foreword and was a great encouragement on the value and worth of this project. We thank John MacArthur, R.C. Sproul, Jr., Don Matzat, and Kim Riddlebarger for their kind endorsements.

And as Christians, we thank the Giver of all these givers—our Lord Jesus Christ, the only man who ever kept all His promises.

Introduction

When pop singer Cheryl Crow asks an apparently befuddled and frustrated companion if he is "strong enough" to be her man, she asks a rather telling question, a question many men would rather just ignore.

Take the guy that lived down the road as just one example. When he moved in, he looked like the kind of guy who had it all: a lovely wife, three beautiful children, a decent career. He even had a Volvo wagon. Less than a year later, however, he left his wife for a teenage girl. Most men his age trade in their older cars to lease a younger model; he traded in his wife. Ironically, the same guy who wasn't "strong enough" to be a man to his wife and children somehow mustered up enough "strength" to be a man to a girl less than half his age. Within weeks he and his young discovery went one way, and his family another.

Not long after, a new family moved into the same house, and they also appeared at first to be living the good life. But like their predecessors, this new family didn't even last a year in the house. Proclaiming one day that he was "tired of doing the family thing," the husband up and left his wife and three children, only to end up marrying another woman and "doing the family thing" with her two children a year later. He wasn't "strong enough" to do the family thing with his own family, so he simply swapped families. Some might think the *house* was jinxed, but we think the problems lie elsewhere.

Weak Yet Strong

What about you? Are you strong enough to be the man God has called you to be? Sure, you may not have left your wife for a teenybopper or swapped families lately. But deep down are you *really* strong enough to be the man God has called you to be? Fundamentally, is your problem that you simply lack strength? Is your real problem that you are hopelessly weak, incapable of being strong enough on your own? When you consider the duties which God has assigned to husbands, do you sometimes think that you were the inspiration for Tom Petty when he sang, "She might need a lot of loving, but she don't need you"?

The bad news is that we can't go it alone as men, whether as husbands or fathers. Left to ourselves we will never be strong enough to be the men that God has called us to be. But the good news of the gospel is that we don't have to go it alone. Someone else has "gone it alone" for us already. Jesus Christ is the One who humbled Himself by becoming a man—the Son of Man—for us. He exercised *His* strength for us by perfectly obeying His Father's every requirement, and paying the penalty we deserved for our rebellion against Him.

He didn't just come to be our supreme moral example. He wasn't merely the archetypical man leading us along the path of our so-called "masculine journey." He actually came to pave the way of salvation for us and to send us along its path, graciously guaranteeing our safe arrival in the end. Because of His strength, we can, along with Paul, confess that when we are weak, then we are strong (2 Cor. 12:10).

Being His Consummate "Yes" Men

This means that when asked whether we are strong enough to be the men that He has called us to be, our answer should always be both "yes" and "no." It should be "no" in that we will never be strong enough on our own. But it should be "yes" because of who Christ is and what He has completed for us already. In fact, it is precisely because we will never be strong enough on our own that we need to find our strength completely in Him. We can do nothing apart from Him, including being "strong enough" to be the men that He wants us to be. But in Christ alone, we have the strength to do all things. Indeed, our every "yes" is in Him.

So if we are ever going to be strong enough to be the men He has called us to be, we must learn what it means to be His consummate "yes men." That is, men who find their every "yes" in Him. We must be men who find their all in all in Him, not men who look to their own "strength" or even their own "promises." Men who look beyond their strength—*beyond their promises*—to His strength and unbroken promise are the very men who, by His grace, trust that He who began a good work in them will perfect it until they are with Him in glory. Only in this way will we truly be strengthened to begin living out that promise in what we think, say, and do in every area of our lives, from loving our wives to raising our children, from participating in the local church to taking a stand for justice in our communities.

As Christian men, we must never rely on our own strength or our own promises, whether they are "kept" or broken. Rather we must trust the *only* Promise Keeper who ever lived: the One who not only kept all of His promises but who also paid the price for each of our broken promises. As Paul put it, all the promises of God find their "yes" in Him (2 Cor. 1:20). In short, we must turn away from ourselves and turn instead to *Him*.

Raising the Standard

Only an exceptional blindness could miss the movement known as Promise Keepers which is sweeping across our nation. This movement is challenging men to come to faith in Christ and to live in faith for Him. And while the movement has stayed the course in many important respects, like any movement, it has, at times, strayed from that course as well.

That's where this book comes in. Without being exhaustive, this book seeks to take a balanced look at the Promise Keepers movement by applauding what it has done well, and by pointing out where, to use the movement's own phrase, it needs to "raise the standard" in the days ahead. In this way Promise Keepers would demonstrate an increasing faithfulness to the full-orbed view of manhood taught in Scripture. Echoing Aslan's cry to the creatures in C. S. Lewis's classic children's tale, *The Last Battle*, our book simply aims to encourage Promise Keepers (the movement) and promise keepers (the men involved) go "further up and further in."

Our heartfelt prayer is that the biblical challenge presented in the pages to follow will result in a "zeal in accord with knowledge" (Rom. 10:2). May those who call themselves "promise keepers," and even those who are honest enough to admit that more often than not they are promise breakers, realize that their *only* strength in life is in the *only* Promise Keeper there ever was—the One who, true to His promise, will make us *strong enough to be His men*.

Part One:
At Its Best

❈ ONE ❈

A Job Well Done

By any standard, the Promise Keepers movement is quite a phenomenon. Beginning modestly with coach Bill McCartney and his long-time friend Dave Wardell, along with 70 other men huddled together in prayer in 1990, Promise Keepers has enjoyed spectacular growth ever since. Just one year later in 1991, the movement enlisted more than fifty times its original number, as some 4,200 men joined forces. The next year of 1992 witnessed explosive growth, as 22,000 heeded the battle cry. From there the forward march continued. In 1993, more than 50,000 rallied to the cause in Boulder, Colorado.[1]

The movement then went national. In 1994, more than 278,000 men made their way to six regional conferences and one national conference. And in 1995, Promise Keepers filled thirteen stadiums, numbering more than 720,000 men.[2] By the time the 1996 conference season is over, Promise Keepers will have sponsored a full-fledged, stadium-styled pastor's conference for more than 70,000 pastors at the Georgia Dome and twenty-two regional conferences scattered across the country, totalling approximately 1.4 million men from all walks of life. In 1997, the movement plans on gathering one million men in Washington D.C. alone, and by the year 2000, the movement hopes to fill 50 stadiums nationwide. The movement has also gone international by establishing

Promise Keepers Canada and has already broadcast at least one conference to over one million listeners in Mexico.[3]

The organization itself also has grown in leaps and bounds. It doubled in size twice in 1995 alone and now boasts several hundred hard-working employees who struggle to keep up with the ever-growing demands placed on them.[4] The national and state offices process hundreds and sometimes thousands of pieces of mail and phone calls each day, especially during the conference season, not to mention the thousands of churches which have tapped into the various resources provided.

The official magazine of the movement is called *New Man*, and it has exploded on the scene. Published by Strang Communications in "partnership" with Promise Keepers, the aesthetically attractive bi-monthly magazine garnered an impressive circulation base of nearly 400,000 in less than its first year and a half, and is expected to top 500,000 before the end of 1996, making it one of the largest paid subscription bases in the country.[5] It already has nearly three times the paid subscribers of *Christianity Today*.

A Movement is Born

No wonder David Blakenhorn, author of the best selling book, *Fatherless America*, calls Promise Keepers "the largest and most important men's movement in the United States today."[6] Richard Halverson, former chaplain to the United States Senate, recently commented that what is taking place through the ministry of the Promise Keepers is one of the most obvious movements of God that he has witnessed in his lifetime.[7] Indeed, friends and foes alike must admit one fact: Promise Keepers has had quite an impact during the last half decade.

It would seem appropriate then to pause for a moment in order to ask what kind of impact the movement has had.

In the pages to follow, we will seek to do just that. In all honesty, we want to conclude with a challenge and encouragement to Promise Keepers to establish a sounder biblical footing for the task that it has undertaken. At the same time, we must start by gladly acknowledging some of the things the Promise Keepers movement has done well. Too often our theological and practical differences are caricatured as being a matter for white hats and black hats to settle in some kind of a doctrinal shootout. Frankly, some of the early critics of Promise Keepers have taken their shots, making a lot of noise and attempting to take no prisoners in the process. In contrast to such Billy-the-Kid tactics, we believe that when interacting with brothers in Christ, firm and pointed criticism is not inconsistent with warm encouragement to do better, and to "strengthen the things which remain" (Rev. 3:2). Our desire is to be irenic, but not at the cost of the truth. Our desire is to articulate the truth without unnecessarily offending our brothers.

Calling a Spade a Spade

So what has the Promise Keepers movement done well? The answer clearly is . . . many things. First, it has seen and correctly identified one of the greatest needs of the hour. The churches of our nation have been overwhelmed by a crisis in masculine confidence, what one Promise Keepers author so poignantly describes as the "sissification" of the church. Men *as men* have been written off by the church—men don't come to church, or if they do come, they do not participate in any significant way. Christian women despise filling the vacuum of leadership, but they feel that they must rise to the occasion. After all, who will do it if they don't? And because the church does not exhibit the biblical model of masculinity, it is not surprising that our culture does not either. Sissies in the church are sissies outside of it too.

The problem can be called by many names. No matter what name it goes by, however, the men of our generation have had what can be described only as a failure of nerve. They have abdicated their responsibilities, and consequently we are in the midst of a tremendous crisis in leadership. Men have fallen, to use the biblical term, into the sin of unbelief. God has always promised tremendous blessings for the households of those who, by His grace, keep His covenant in faithful reliance upon Him; but, to be blunt, we as men no longer believe Him. We have fallen so far away from His Word that we no longer know what God's covenant with a household even *is*—how He has promised to be not only our God but the God of our children after us (Act 2:39). Having failed to know His covenant promise to us and our children, we have also failed to understand the nature of covenant reality all around us.

Until we recover this understanding of covenant masculinity, we have no way of comprehending the cultural chaos surrounding us. The clamor of voices rises higher every day. Pundits on television point us in all kinds of directions that we might know the way out. *This way, no that.* How is it that we have come to be ruled by such clamor? In order to answer this question, we must probe our wounds deeply. The pain is excruciating, which is not surprising, given the extent of our condition. For placing the issues of biblical masculinity and male abdication at the top of our current agenda, Promise Keepers deserves our warmest thanks and deepest gratitude.

Sticks and Stones

In addition, Promise Keepers has made the right enemies, and on the proper scale. The secular feminists and activists are understandably nervous when they see droves of professing believers with traditional values rallying together across the country. Not surprisingly, they have made their displeasure known. After observing the Promise Keepers conference at Dallas, Texas in 1995, for instance, a female producer for Swiss TV said that the movement was nothing more than Moslem fundamentalism in its subjugation of women. Apparently, she wasn't listening when the men who packed out Texas Stadium were pointedly and repeatedly told that the way to *lead* their wives and children was by *serving* them. As another example, radical feminists rented planes to fly above Folsom Stadium during the 1994 conference in Boulder, Colorado, displaying taunting messages such as "Only Weak Men Fear Strong Women," and "Smart Women Don't Buy Your Promises," and "Promise Keepers, Loosers [*sic*], Weepers." Aside from failing third-grade spelling, these feminist critics have missed the whole point of Promise Keepers. If they want that kind of strength, they can have O. J. If they want the wisdom of this world, they will come to regret it. The message of the cross is "foolishness" to those who are *perishing* (1 Cor. 1:18).

It is foolishness to them precisely because the "natural man" cannot understand spiritual things, which, in the words of Paul, "are spiritually discerned" (2 Cor. 2:14); hence, those without the Spirit cannot properly discern them. To attempt to view the Promise Keepers movement through the spectacles of naturalism blurs the movement. Not surprisingly, then, many critics of a political bent have unfairly criticized Promise Keepers for constituting some kind of front for a hidden political agenda, when, if the truth be known, the movement has done nothing to give anyone any reason to suspect it of having any political agenda, let alone a hidden one.

Some, for example, have pointed to the plans Promise Keepers has had on the drawing boards to assemble more than one million men in the nation's capital in 1997 and have insinuated that Promise Keepers borrowed the idea from Louis Farrakhan's "Million Man March" in 1995. Just because Promise Keepers plans on assembling men in Washington, D.C. after Farrakhan did so, does not mean that Promise Keepers has any relationship to a particular political cause. In fact, Promise Keepers had its plans on the drawing board and publicly announced those plans years *before* Farrakhan "stole the show." But even more importantly, Promise Keepers is not planning to descend on the nation's capital to *protest* anything. It is not going to protest, but to *pray.* It is not going to engage in vitriolic and separatist rhetoric, but to pray peaceably and exhibit unity. It is not going to proclaim Christ as some kind of lesser prophet, but to exalt Him as the Prophet, Priest, and King—the Redeemer of His people.

Aside from the superficial connection between the "Million Man March" and the Promise Keepers time of prayer, the movement has no political overtones. It supports no political party. It endorses no candidates for office. It makes no contributions to candidates. And for good reason: Promise Keepers works hard to avoid the political fray. Politics divides, and Promise Keepers seeks to unite Christian men of all sizes, shapes, and colors. While the leadership of Promise Keepers would be the first to tell you that the gospel has cultural and political implications, they would also tell you that the key is *not legislation but transformation,* not change from without, but change from within. As men truly turn to God and then live out their Christian commitment in their marriages, homes, churches, workplaces, and communities, the cultural landscape will be transformed. Promise Keepers simply seeks to facilitate that transformation.

And *that* is what radical feminists and activists find distasteful. But instead of debating the issues, they have resorted to *ad hominem* arguments and abusive epithets. They have whined that Promise Keepers conferences promote patriarchy by excluding women. But where were all the men when some of those very same critics orchestrated the United Nations Fourth World Conference on Women in Beijing last year? Not that men really wanted to attend lesbian flirtation workshops and the like, but the jealousy and inconsistency of these critics is remarkable.

Admittedly, secularists have grounds for being jealous and inconsistent when it comes to Promise Keepers. As a movement, Promise Keepers has surpassed anything secularists could ever dream of, even when their secular conferences are supported directly or indirectly by worldwide tax dollars. Feminists could not fill stadiums across America, so they huddle together behind the Great Wall of China. Try as they might in denying the obvious, unbelievers can only fill stadiums to watch people chase a ball—never an idea.

Escaping the Secular Ghetto

And this fact raises yet another point secularists would just rather forget: far from constituting the escapist opiate of the masses, religious motivation remains one of the most potent cultural forces ever known. That this fact has been ignored in our public discourse for more than a generation has not altered the situation. Men and women are inescapably religious. When that impulse is repressed or foolishly ignored, as it has been in our post-modern culture, we shouldn't be surprised when an explosion follows. Promise Keepers represents tens of thousands of Christian men who have escaped the cultural ghetto which secularists reserved for them, and who are now standing out in public where everyone can see them. Many of these men simply seek to return (rightly) to the old paths, to a time when the world made more sense than it does now.

We rejoice, then, that the Promise Keepers phenomenon demonstrates a genuine spiritual hunger, a thirst for wholeness, a God-given desire for something more than the ho-hum Christianity to which many have become accustomed in our day. Our religious establishment has consistently underestimated the spiritual interests of men. Because of this, men have often been written off as uninterested, when they were simply uninterested in the feminized way the truth of the gospel was being presented. This phenomenon shows that Christian men in our nation do have a deep-seated interest in spiritual things. The potential clearly exists to present the Christian worldview in a way that does not relegate the American male to the back pews.

Putting Off the Old Man

Undeniably, scores of lives have been dramatically touched by God's grace as a result of the outreach of Promise Keepers. By the thousands, men are standing up to be counted *as men* in every area of their lives. To its credit, Promise Keepers has challenged men not only to acknowledge that Christ is Lord of their individual lives, but of their marriages, families, churches, careers, and communities as well. Christ is not just Lord of our hearts; He is Lord of all. And Promise Keepers is to be applauded for helping certain segments of the church begin to recover this long-lost truth.

While the hype of a Promise Keepers conference may outstrip its hope in some cases, at the same time many men have experienced true conversion through the outreach of Promise Keepers. By God's grace, they are displaying the fruit of that conversion in their lives. Many professing Christians have recognized the sinfulness of their ways and, by God's grace, have confessed their sin and have returned to the straight and narrow. Says one wife of a promise keeper, "I don't know what happened to my husband, but I don't want the old one back." Her story could be told hundreds, if not thousands, of times over.

Hitting Racism Hard

Just as impressively, Promise Keepers has demonstrated no shortage of courage by going toe to toe with the sin of racism that has divided the American church far too long. The church should be ashamed that racism has sometimes been more virulent within her walls than outside them. White evangelicals, for example, are more likely to complain about African-American or Hispanic neighbors than whites who are unchurched.[8] This situation is a travesty and unmitigated ugliness.

On this issue, Promise Keepers has cut men to the quick with the demands of God's Word. Racism is sin, sin of the most grievous sort. The church owes a debt of gratitude to Promise Keepers for confronting its members with the fact that we cannot claim to love God whom we have not seen and continue hating our neighbors next door simply because they reflect light differently. To hate those made in the image of God, ultimately, is to hate the One who made them. It's really that simple, and it's really that sinful.

Getting Out the Word

Whether addressing racism in particular or the need for repentance in general, Promise Keepers has come a long way in a relatively short period of time. One reason the movement has made such great strides so rapidly is the incredible communications and public relations machinery it has put in place since its inception. Far from being a point of criticism, as some are wont to make it, the communications machinery Promise Keepers has assembled should be admired and used to the greater glory of God. Promise Keepers is building bridges to our generation in a way that is being seen and understood. For that, the movement is to be heartily commended.

This communications machinery of the Promise Keepers works in tandem with the impressive organizational structure Promise Keepers has developed. Of course, Promise Keepers is best known for its highly visible conferences scattered throughout the country. While, as noted above, Promise Keepers began with a prayer meeting in 1990, in 1991, it began developing an annual theme around which the conferences would revolve.

The 1991 Boulder conference focused on the theme "Where Are the Men?" In 1992, the Boulder conference asked the all-important question, "What Makes a Man?" The 1993 Boulder conference turned to the task of learning to work together "Face to Face," while the seven conferences in 1994 taught men to "Seize the Moment." The 13 regional conferences in 1995 challenged men to "Raise the Standard," and the twenty-two conferences scheduled for this year are encouraging men to "Break Down the Walls."

But the conferences are not the only "events" Promise Keepers hosts throughout the year. To prepare men for the conferences and to ensure that the conferences are well attended, Promise Keepers hosts mini-conferences, what it calls "Wake Up Calls" across the country throughout the year. In 1994, Promise Keepers hosted 120 Wake Up Calls, and in 1995, it hosted approximately 300.[9] Wake Up Calls serve three purposes: (1) to "build momentum for the large Promise Keepers' conferences," (2) to "bring men together who have a heart for men's ministry," and (3) to "stir men's hearts about needs within their community—to encourage them to get together, pray, and form small groups."[10]

Promise Keepers also hosts "Men's Ministry Leadership Seminars" throughout the country. Over 45,000 men attended such conferences in 1994, while well in excess of that number attended them in 1995. Intended for pastors, lay leaders, and "any man who has a heart for men's ministry," the typical Men's Ministry Leadership Seminar "examines the current men's movement, offers answers to the issues men face today and provides proven methods for developing an effective men's ministry."[11]

The organizational structure of Promise Keepers is not just reflected in its visible conferences, Wake Up Calls, and Men's Ministry Leadership Seminars; Promise Keepers is also a well-organized institution in its own right, deepening its contact with local churches through what it calls its Point Man/Ambassador Network. Point Men (or Key Men, as they sometimes are called) are liaisons between Promise Keepers and the local church. Point Men may be pastors or men's ministry leaders of the church or simply laymen, but they serve as the local contact between Promise Keepers and the local church and vice versa. To fulfill this role, Point Men work with their respective Ambassador, a man who works to promote the values of Promise Keepers to the community and its churches. Ambassadors must be acknowledged leaders, able to represent Promise Keepers' mission with faithfulness and maturity, and be approved by the National Ambassador Office.

Though Point Men and Ambassadors may be similar in terms of their giftedness, Promise Keepers views them as having very different missions. As one brochure puts it, "Point Men are the vital link between Promise Keepers and the local church," whereas "Ambassadors are the critical relational link between Point Men and Promise Keepers."[12] Thus, Point Men focus on discipling men to become godly leaders in their churches, while Ambassadors focus on the community, devoting themselves to lifting up and equipping Point Men in their effectiveness within the church.

The Point Men report to Ambassadors, who, in turn, report to the local Task Force, a group of ethnically and denominationally diverse men who have met for prayer for 3-6 months and who have signed and returned the "Affiliation Agreement" to Promise Keepers, along with the funds needed to purchase an orientation kit. This orientation kit more fully acquaints the members of the Task Force with the mission and values of Promise Keepers and allows the Task Force to use the name and registered logo of Promise Keepers on a limited basis for the purpose of accomplishing the well-defined local mission. The Task Force does three things: (1) it organizes local events such as initial orientation breakfasts, Wake Up Calls, and Men's Ministry Leadership Seminars; (2) it organizes the local Point Man/Ambassador network; and (3) it, along with other task forces, helps organize statewide events, working with the State Steering Committee to that end. The State Steering Committee receives guidance and direction from Regional Directors who, in turn, receive their guidance and direction from the National Office.

With a structure like that, no one would dare accuse the Promise Keepers of needing to get organized. Peter Drucker couldn't have done better!

Let's Be Objective About This

Though the list of commendations could go on and on, the point is obvious to any impartial observer: the Promise Keepers movement has done many things well and should be commended in many respects for a job well done. In many ways the movement is, well, . . . full of promise.

Nevertheless, there is still some cause for concern. In the pages to follow, we will take a look at some of those concerns so that together, we can learn how to become true men of promise. But why not rally around what the movement has done so very well and just leave well enough alone? The answer is that our standard is not what men say, but rather, what God says. As Christians, we must listen to Him and bring everything we believe and do into submission to His Lordship and into conformity with the standard of His Word. And we shouldn't take offense if others come along to help us out. That's what being on the same team is all about.

However, the fact that we believe ourselves to be on the same team does not mean we believe our criticisms to be of minor importance. If they were minor, it would be best to leave the whole thing alone. No good reason can be given for troubling the church of Christ over trivial matters. As you will see, our concerns lie right at the heart of the gospel, and we are obligated to express them plainly. When the gospel is being threatened or blurred, the stakes are too high to sacrifice love on the altar of civility.

Just think of Peter and Barnabas, both of whom were corrected by Paul face to face because, in Paul's words, "they were not straightforward about the truth of the gospel" (Gal. 2:14). They erred publicly, and Paul firmly corrected them there and then. The Bible does not so much as hint that they thought themselves to be beyond such correction. And regardless, they needed to be corrected.

Neither is there any indication that Paul himself was put off when those who resided in the New Testament city of Berea refused to take his word for it as he taught them the Scriptures from day to day. Instead, they actually had the audacity to compare Scriptures to what the inspired apostle taught "to see whether these things were so" (Acts 17:11). Far from condemning the Bereans for refusing to take Paul's word as gospel truth, Scripture actually commends them for their "eagerness" and "noble-mindedness" in examining for themselves everything he taught them. Like the Bereans of old, we need to demonstrate the same eagerness and noble-mindedness today by examining the Scriptures to see whether the things we hear and read are so—no matter who is doing the teaching, how many books he has sold or how many radio stations carry his broadcasts.

Then there was Apollos, "an eloquent man" who was "mighty in the Scriptures" (Acts 18:24). But he had a slight problem: he had the wrong view of baptism. Instead of ignoring his error or treating it as unimportant, we are told that when Priscilla and Aquila heard him, "they took him aside and explained to him the way of God more accurately" (v. 26). The result? The man mighty in the Scriptures became even mightier, and his ministry flourished (v. 28).

If Peter, Barnabas, Paul, and Apollos took no offense at this enterprise, neither should we. After all, we are on the same team. We need each other to help us focus on our divine game plan. Our purpose here is simply to encourage the Promise Keepers, accurately and charitably, to build on a more biblical foundation. We begin, then, with a look at the gospel according to the Promise Keepers.

---

[1] Anon., "Promise Keepers Fact Sheet (10/3/95)," p. 1.

[2] *Ibid.*

[3] Anon., "Promise Keepers Goes North," *New Man*, March/April, 1996, vol. 3, no. 2, p. 19; Anon., "Texas Stadium Filled With Men—Filled With Glory," (n.d.), p. 1.

[4] "Promise Keepers Fact Sheet (10/3/95)," p. 2.

[5] Kirk Bane, Strang Communications letter dated October 9, 1995.

[6] Joseph P. Shapiro, "Heavenly Promises," *U.S. News & World Report*, October 2, 1995, p. 68.

[7] Quoted by Randy Phillips, October 27, 1995 press conference, Dallas, Texas.

[8] George Gallup and James Castelli, *The People's Religion* (New York, NY: MacMillan, 1989), p. 188, quoted in Michael Horton, *The Law of Perfect Freedom* (Chicago, IL: Moody Press, 1993), p. 156.

[9] Ken Walker, "300 Wake Up Calls Planned for 1995," *New Man*, March/April, 1995, vol. 2, no. 2, p. 74.

[10] *Ibid.*, quoting Promise Keepers' President of National Ministries, Rick Kingham.

[11] Rod Cooper, "1995 Men's Ministry Leadership Seminars" (Fall 1995).

[12] Promise Keepers Brochure, "How You Can Establish Promise Keepers in Your Region," n.d.

Part Two:
Some Cause For Concern

❀ TWO ❀

The Gospel of Guyhood

Promise Keepers is commonly described as an "evangelical" movement. That description, as recently noted by David Wells, has lost much of its original meaning. The term originally meant something solid: that which revolved around the *evangel*—the gospel—as revealed in Scripture. Today, however, the term means something far different. As proof, consider how seldom the term *evangelical* even stands by itself anymore. Nowadays, we rarely speak of someone as being *evangelical*. Instead, we speak of people as being *conservative* evangelicals, *mainline* evangelicals, *feminist* evangelicals, and so on.

In a day and age when we, in Wells' words, have made "no place for truth," we seem to have made place only for our experiences. Sadly, what oftentimes unites self-professing evangelicals today is not necessarily the truth of the evangel, as much as the rush of their feelings.

So when Promise Keepers claims to be an evangelical movement, we need to pause and ask *what kind of evangelical movement it is*. And that is simply another way of asking what kind of gospel it proclaims.

Come Out, Come Out, Wherever You Are

At least one newspaper apparently couldn't discern any distinctive gospel in the Promise Keepers movement when it recently asked: "Is the fastest growing Christian movement in America led by men who won't, or can't, define what the term 'Christian' means?"[1] Of course, by failing to define the term *Christian* as clearly as it should, Promise Keepers has also failed to define what lies at the heart of true Christianity. This heart is the gospel, which, according to Paul, is "the power of God for salvation to everyone who believes" (Rom. 1:16).

One need not listen to Promise Keepers speakers long, or read what some in the movement have written, before realizing that the "gospel" Paul repeatedly speaks of gets little, if any, air time. As opposed to the gospel proclaimed throughout the Bible, the "gospel" proclaimed by some Promise Keepers spokesmen is, with a few notable exceptions, nothing short of moralism, pure and simple. To be saved, we are told, we must *do*.

The president of Promise Keepers, Randy Phillips, himself has quoted evangelist Greg Laurie in *Seven Promises of a Promise Keeper*, the book defining the Promise Keepers movement, by writing that men "need to *do* 5 things to become a part of God's family," and the list includes "living to please Him."[2] He also tells Christian men that they must seize the moment, a process which, he claims, "starts by making some promises—promises we intend to keep."[3]

Gregg Lewis, another Promise Keepers author, wrote an official book of the movement entitled *The Power of a Promise Kept*, a title which implies that our human promises have a power inherent in them which, when kept, transform our lives. Lest anyone think otherwise, Phillips sets the tone for the book by asserting in its introduction: "If you commit to Him, He will transform you."[4] Notice the if-then logic of this assertion. *If* you commit, *then* God will transform you. "Commit to what?" you ask.

"The seven promises," comes the reply. Bill McCartney plainly says so.

> . . . we start by committing our lives to Jesus Christ and becoming a new creation (see 2 Cor. 5:17). Then we make the kinds of commitments to growth embodied in the seven promises covered in this book, and we make them to other men who will hold us accountable and give us the benefit of their experience and wisdom. As we do this, our thoughts, words, decisions, and actions *will change* over time.[5]

Randy Phillips has also spoken of the transforming power of the seven promises:

> [These promises] are meant to guide us toward the life of Christ and to *transform* us within so that we might see transformation in our homes, among our friends, in our churches, and, ultimately, in our nation.[6]

Phillips leaves no doubt that for him, sanctification is a *quid pro quo* process. We do our thing. Then and only then does God do His. And behind it all are the seven promises. Make these promises, and if you really mean them, your life will be transformed from within.

Perfected by the Flesh?

By so teaching, Promise Keepers has claimed something for the seven promises not even the ten commandments can do. Not even the "holy and righteous and good" moral law of God as summarized by the ten commandments can transform our lives (Rom. 7:12). Among other things, the moral law was given by God to convict us of our *inability* to keep it perfectly, in order to drive us to Christ as the only One who ever kept it perfectly for us (Rom. 7:7; Gal. 3:23-25).

And even after driving us to Christ, the moral law of God does not transform us in our Christian life. It does not and cannot make us righteous. It only provides a pattern of righteousness for us (1 Jn. 3:4). It functions like a ruler. Just as it would be difficult to approximate a straight line without a ruler, so it would be impossible, to approximate a life of righteousness without the divine standard of righteousness by which we are measured. The moral law is that standard.

But never does that law transform us. Now if the perfect moral law of God, written by His very hand, provides no power to transform us, can our merely human promises fare any better? If the *ten commandments* cannot transform us, how can the *seven promises*? Paul teaches us that what the law was powerless to do, God did by sending us His Son (Rom. 8:3).

By suggesting that our works (our promises) can transform us, the Promise Keepers movement has blurred the purity of the gospel. The gospel deals a crushing blow to human pride by teaching us that our works never transform us. Only *God* transforms. And He does so only by His grace alone through faith alone on account of what Christ alone has done for us.

When it comes to being put right with God, grace and works are like oil and water; they simply don't mix. As Paul unequivocally taught,

> He saved us, not on the basis of the deeds which we have done in righteousness, but according to His mercy, by the washing and regeneration and renewing of the Holy Spirit, whom He poured out on us richly through Jesus Christ our Savior, that being justified by His grace we might be made heirs according to the hope of eternal life (Titus 3:5-7).

And after being "justified by His grace," we do not perfect ourselves in the flesh. To miss this truth is to miss Paul's heartfelt burden throughout the book of Galatians. We do not begin in the Spirit and end in the flesh:

> You foolish Galatians, who has bewitched you, before whose eyes Jesus Christ was publicly portrayed as crucified? This is the only thing I want to find out from you: did you receive the Spirit by the works of the Law, or by hearing with faith? Are you so foolish? Having begun by the Spirit, are you now being perfected by the flesh? (Gal. 3:1-3).

Paul asks a rhetorical question, the answer to which is obvious. As Christians, we do not begin the new life by the power and work of the Holy Spirit, only to add the finishing touches ourselves by our commitments or efforts. Salvation does not begin with God and end with man. Yet the message proclaimed by the Promise Keepers is permeated with the notion that God does His thing only when we do our thing. And the "thing" we are to do is to make and keep the seven promises. We are saved and sanctified by law, Promise Keepers style.

Promise Keepers Then and Now

That this view can be taught and accepted as evangelical Christianity is regrettable because it flies in the face of the evangel itself. We must remember that Christ in His earthly ministry sought to disabuse those in His day who had the notion that they somehow could be put right with Him by keeping God's law.

Consider for a moment the rich young ruler who came to Christ, asking what he needed to do to be saved. Christ told Him that all He had to do was to obey the perfect law of God. Instead of getting the point and admitting his inability to do so on his own, the rich young ruler actually replied that he had kept the law. And he had not begun his supposed law-keeping as a full grown man after attending a Christian pep rally at the Roman Colosseum, but allegedly from the time he was a youth. Christ, knowing better, forcefully reminded him that he had not obeyed at least one of the commandments, given his greedy and covetous heart. He did this by telling the rich young ruler to go and sell all his possessions (Lk. 18:18-23). The rich young ruler thought that he had kept the law of God, only to be reminded that he had not *really* kept it at all. He went away sad, realizing his failure, not puffed up in thinking that he had passed Law-Keeping 101.

But what about you? Do you, like the rich young ruler, really think that you are keeper of the law? How about the seven promises? For the sake of simplicity, take just one of the promises for now, say the third one, which says, "*A Promise Keeper is committed to practicing spiritual, moral, ethical, and sexual purity.*"[7] Do you really *keep* this promise? Even more to the point, *can* you really keep it? Are you pure—really pure—in and of yourself? Even charitably assuming for argument's sake that you are spiritually, morally, and ethically pure, are you sexually pure?

"Sure I am pure. I have never actually committed adultery," you proudly say. Congratulations! Now turn to Matthew 5 and see what Christ says about sexual purity. While refraining from outward adultery is part of what it means to be sexually pure, this is not all it means. It is not enough to refrain from outward adultery. True sexual purity also requires that you *never* lust. Christ Himself put it this way to the "promise keepers" of His day:

> You have heard that it was said, "You shall not commit adultery"; but I say to you, that everyone who looks on a woman to lust for her has committed adultery with her already in his heart (Matt. 5:27-28).

Admittedly, not every temptation is a lust. As Martin Luther once quipped, we can't keep the birds from flying over our heads but we can keep them from making a nest in our hair. Yet even with this helpful distinction between temptation and lust in mind, can you truthfully say that you have stopped all the birds from nesting? Listen long enough, and you're bound to hear some chirping.

Christ's whole point in the Sermon on the Mount was to demonstrate that outward obedience, though commendable, is not all God requires of us. He requires inward obedience as well. Being sexually pure requires that we never lust. So what are we who are so prone to lust to do?

Guilty as Charged

We must start by freely acknowledging that we fail miserably to measure up to God's perfect moral standards. We must admit that we are far from loving God and our neighbors as we ought (Lk. 10:25-28). We have violated more than one of God's commandments and, in the words of James, we are "lawbreakers"—we violate the entire law (Js. 2:10) before a Judge who doesn't just look on the outside but who also weighs our hearts (1 Sam. 16:7; Prov. 21:2).

If our Lord's Sermon on the Mount teaches us anything, it teaches us that the demands of the law are not satisfied when we avoid certain outward actions. Those same demands reach deep within us and prick our hearts as well. We may not have committed outward adultery, but we all have lusted. And that, Christ says, is a violation of the seventh commandment (Matt. 5:27-28).

Of course, we violate all of the commandments in what we think, what we say, and what we do. Idolaters, false worshippers, blasphemers, Sabbath breakers, rebels, murderers, adulterers, thieves, liars, and the covetous are not just outside the church halls. They also fill the pews. Your pew, to be more specific. Tall or short, fat or skinny, young or old, we have all broken God's holy law and continue to do so every day in thought, word, and deed.

Not only do we sin each day, but we do so because we are sinners by nature. To say that we are sinners by nature is simply to say that the guilt of Adam's original sin was imputed or credited to us as his heirs; in the words of Paul, we "were made sinners" through Adam's disobedience (Rom. 5:19). David, you will recall, reiterated this truth when he wrote that we were "brought forth in iniquity" (Ps. 51:5) and "estranged from the womb" (Ps. 58:3).

Why was Adam's original sin credited to us? For the simple reason that he acted as our legal representative or covenant head. When your Congressman votes in favor of a particular bill, he acts on behalf of his constituents at home. In a similar way, Adam's sin was a sin on behalf of his constituents, his heirs. He represented us all. Thus, we, as His heirs, were counted to have done through Him what He did (Rom. 5:12, 16-19). While we didn't personally eat of the forbidden fruit ourselves, we were counted sinners as Adam's offspring and bear the sinful nature, depravity, and corruption which flow from his sin. We are all therefore promise-breakers by nature.

No one is righteous, no one does good (Rom. 3:9, 12), not even those who pride themselves on being more religious than the next guy. Even the apparent "good" we do is but "filthy rags" in God's sight (Is. 64:6).[8] Indeed, no one is excluded from this indictment since all have sinned and continually fall short of the glory of God (Rom. 3:23). All are under the curse for failing to fulfil the righteous demands of God's law perfectly (Deut. 27:26; Gal. 3:10; Js. 2:10). Make no mistake: we are cursed sinners since we were made sinners through Adam's disobedience, and because of that, we continue to sin every day. While the grace of God meets us in this condition and frees the believer from the power of sin, in no way does God's grace remove us from the presence of our remaining corruptions. We have to deal with them daily (1 Pet. 2:11), and no amount of promising can change that.

God Doesn't Grade on a Curve

And yet, if we would be saved, the perfectly holy and righteous God of Scripture requires that we not only be sinless, but that we also be perfectly righteous. We are to be holy as He is holy (Lev. 11:44-45; 1 Pet. 1:15-16), to be perfect as He is perfect (Matt. 5:48), to imitate Him (Eph. 5:1). Contrary to popular belief, God doesn't grade on a curve. He requires that we be perfect, not in some watered down sense, but in the same way that He is perfect.

But how can we ever imitate Him? How can we ever be as perfectly holy as an all-holy God? How can we ever be sinless since we have already sinned and continue to do so in thought, word, and deed? How can we ever be perfectly righteous if we are sinners by nature? In short, how can we ever become right with God?

Is it impossible? That's what the disciples once thought when, in the context of the encounter between Christ and the rich young ruler, they despairingly cried out, "Then who can be saved?" Christ comforted them by changing their focus. Instead of focusing on man, they needed to focus on God. Rather than looking at what *man* must do to be saved, they needed to look at what *God* does for man. Salvation, according to Christ, is *impossible with men*, but is *possible with God and only with God* (Lk. 18:26-27).

Man, in other words, cannot save himself. If he is to be saved at all, He must be saved by God. From beginning to end, salvation is from the Lord alone. What is impossible with us is possible with God. The rich young ruler didn't get it. Neither did the Pharisees. God requires nothing short of perfection.

The Great Exchange

Though God requires perfection, the perfection He requires can't come from us. It must come from another. And the good news of the gospel is that it does! It comes from Christ.

We don't have to earn God's favor since Christ has done so for us already. Because of who Christ is and what He has done for us already, God credits our sin to Him and then credits His righteousness to us. His righteousness is simply *given* to us and is credited to our account. Think of it this way. Apart from Christ, we were totally indebted and completely bankrupt. We had no money to pay the enormous debt that we owed to God. But at the right time, Christ stepped in our place, assumed our debt, and paid it off for us. Then, not content with merely paying off our debt, He also deposited His infinite wealth in our account. This transaction can be understood as the great exchange. It is what Paul had in mind when he told the Corinthians that God made Christ "who knew no sin to be sin for us that we might become the righteousness of God in Him" (2 Cor. 5:21).

Why did Christ have to take on our sin and to credit us with His righteousness? To satisfy the double demand the law of God makes on us as sinners: first, the demand that we perfectly obey its precepts; and second, the demand that we fully pay the penalty we deserve for having violated its precepts. Left to ourselves, we could never meet this double demand. We could neither perfectly obey the law nor fully pay the penalty for violating it. But the glorious good news of the gospel is that Christ, acting in our place and on our behalf, has already satisfied the double demand of the law for us.

How so? Just as Adam acted as our covenant head or legal representative by plunging us into sin and death, so Christ, as "the last Adam," acted as our covenant head or legal representative by lifting us into righteousness and life

(Rom. 5:12-21). In our place and on our behalf, Christ perfectly obeyed God's law, thereby satisfying its first demand. Then He fully suffered the penalty of the law against sin, thereby satisfying its second demand. Through Him, *we* have actually satisfied the double demand of the law.

From Rags to Robes

What a tremendous truth! Because of what Christ has done for us both in His life and death, we can, along with Isaiah, proclaim that our "righteousness and strength" are "only in the Lord." In Him alone, we as "the offspring of Israel will be justified, and will glory" (Is. 45:24-25). As Jeremiah proclaims, He is the "Lord our righteousness" (Jer. 23:6). Paul joins this chorus as well when he declares that Christ is our "righteousness, holiness, and redemption" (1 Cor. 1:30).

Like Adam and Eve in the post-fall Garden, we, too, once stood naked in our shame, guilt, and wickedness. But as with Adam and Eve, God clothed us. This time He also provided clothing far better than man-made fig leaf suits designed to hide our shame, guilt, and wickedness. This time, He gave us His own clothes—the "garments of salvation." We are robed in His righteousness (Is. 61:10)!

Because God has removed our "filthy garments" from us, "taken [our] iniquity away" from us, and clothed us "with festal robes" (Zech. 3:4), our justification is based on what He has done for us, not what we have done ourselves. Along with Paul, we should confess that we want to be

found in Christ not having a righteousness of [our] own . . . but that which is through faith in Christ, the righteousness which comes from God on the basis of faith (Phil. 3:9).

So instead of making promises in the hope that something will happen inside us, we must abandon all reliance upon ourselves and our promises. We must cast ourselves completely on Christ. While Promise Keepers speakers and authors constantly look for something to happen *in us downstream* based on what we do, the good news of the gospel is that something has happened *for us already.* That good news does not need any human supplement.

When all is said and done, we have only to fall on our knees in praise and thanks to God for freely and graciously saving us by His grace. The law came, in part, to terrorize and condemn us in our wickedness. But Christ came to fulfill its demands for us. In our place and on our behalf, He fully paid our penalty for violating the law and perfectly obeyed its every precept.

The answer to our predicament is not to pull ourselves up by our own bootstraps. The answer is not that God, in the words of the Maranatha! Promise Band, "just needs a few good men," since, among the sons of Adam, there is no good man (Rom. 3:9-26). The answer is found in the only Good Man there ever was—Jesus Christ.

We must not look within, at our own works or promises. Rather, we must look outside of ourselves—beyond our promises to Christ. He is the *only* Promise Keeper there ever was; He is the One who not only perfectly kept His promise to save us from all eternity, but who also fully paid the price for each of our broken promises. Indeed, the promises of God find their "yes" in Him (2 Cor. 1:20).

The answer is not what *Newsweek*, in evaluating the Promise Keepers movement, called "the gospel of guyhood." The answer is the gospel of Christ. The answer is *Christ*. We must turn away from ourselves and turn instead to Him. It is high time for the Promise Keepers to recover a clear statement of this long lost truth. For it is none other than the gospel.

¹ Quoted by Martin and Deidre Bobgan, *Psycho Heresy Awareness Letter*, July/August, 1995, vol. 3, no. 4, p. 8.

² Randy Phillips, *Seven Promises of a Promise Keeper* (Colorado Springs, CO: Focus on the Family Publishing, 1994), p. 10, emphasis added (hereafter "*SPPK*"), adapting Greg Laurie, *New Believers Growth Book* (Riverside, CA: Harvest Ministries, 1985), p. 8.

³ *Ibid.*, p. 8.

⁴ *The Power of a Promise Kept* (Colorado Springs, CO: Focus on the Family Publishing, 1995), p. 3 (hereafter "*TPPK*").

⁵ *SPPK*, pp. 206-207; reprinted in *New Man*, "The Power of a Promise," March/April, vol. 2, no. 2, 1995, p. 73.

⁶ *Ibid.*, p. 9, emphasis added.

⁷ *Ibid.*, p. 8.

⁸ The phrase "filthy rags" is literally translated "menstrual cloths."

❖ THREE ❖

The Tea Party Mentality

Promise Keepers author and speaker Tony Evans hits the nail on the head when he attributes the crisis of masculinity in American culture, at least in part, to the feminization of the American male.

> I am convinced that the primary cause of this national crisis is the feminization of the American male. When I say *feminization*, I am not talking about sexual preference. I'm trying to describe a misunderstanding of manhood that has produced a nation of "sissified" men who abdicate their role as spiritually pure leaders, thus forcing women to fill the vacuum.[1]

We do have a nation of sissified men, men Evans has no problem describing as having been duped by a deceitful model of true masculinity. The critical question, however, is whether Promise Keepers is doing something about the problem it has identified so astutely or whether it unwittingly is part of the problem.

Of course, the Promise Keepers movement has done something valuable to address the problem. By challenging men to take back the reigns in their marriages, homes, churches, and communities, Promise Keepers has separated the men from the sissies. But even when it has taken two steps forward in this regard, it unfortunately has, in some respects, taken three steps back.

Although the gospel preached by Promise Keepers sometimes verges on the gospel of guyhood, at other times in the name of guyhood, Promise Keepers unwittingly goes in the *opposite* direction by feminizing men in the name of the gospel. Not only does the movement miss the point of the gospel, at times it also misses the meaning of true, biblical masculinity.

In the Beginning

To see why this is the case, we need to go back to the dawn of creation. God made man, and God made woman. The man was not the woman, and the woman was not the man. When God created the man, He put him in the Garden to accomplish several tasks (Gen. 2:7, 15). He then brought the woman to the man to help him accomplish his God-given tasks (2:18, 20-22).

In other words, the man was first made to be task-oriented and then, from a human viewpoint, relationship-oriented, having been brought into relationship with the woman to accomplish his divinely entrusted tasks. By contrast the woman was created first and foremost to be relationship-oriented; that is, to exist in relationship with the man. She was made for him in order to help him accomplish the tasks entrusted to him by God.

What went on in the Garden is part of the fabric of creation and provides a pattern for married couples today as Paul, under inspiration of the Holy Spirit, readily affirms:

> For man does not originate from woman, but woman from man; for indeed man was not created for the woman's sake, but woman for the man's sake (1 Cor. 11:8-9; *cf.* 1 Tim. 2:13).

According to Paul, what was true in the Garden was true in the Roman Empire. It is also true today. The man and the woman were made at different times and for different purposes. This basic biblical truth explains why men and women are different. They were made that way.

Even Hollywood understands this inherent difference between the sexes. Think of the typical movie written for men (*The Terminator*) and the typical movie written for women (*Fried Green Tomatoes*). In the typical men's movie, the plot is rather simple: the man is out to do something, and if there is a relationship at all, it is a subplot—something brought in from the side. By contrast, the typical woman's movie features the relationship itself as the main plot. Despite its rebellion against God in other areas, not even Hollywood can escape the fabric of creation as woven by God.

Some Promise Keepers authors recognize the inherent differences between the sexes. In *The Awesome Power of Shared Beliefs*, Vice President of Ministry Advancement for the Promise Keepers, E. Glenn Wagner, has correctly observed that *"(m)en are highly task oriented and not very relationship oriented."*[2] Others have said or written the same thing.

But instead of seeing that the differences between the sexes reflect the way we were created by God, Promise Keepers authors and speakers view it as a weakness, something that needs to be changed in men. Consistently, we are told that men need to be less task-oriented and more relationship-oriented, that they need to be more like women in this regard. Here's how one author put it:

> If you look through the shelves of your local bookstore you'll find very few books on mentoring, and they are almost all written by women. Why? Because the core of mentoring is a relationship between mentor and protege, and women instinctively understand relationship. Men generally think in terms of activity, which is why so many men struggle with beginning a mentoring relationship.[3]

Promise Keepers author Robert Hicks laments that "the problem" with men is that they talk to women when they should be talking with each other. He goes on to say,

> We can hide in the closets of competition, use emotional walls to protect us, or flee the reality of our deepest fears, but when we do, we flee from our own manhood. The close, nonsexual presence of other men will affirm our manhood more than anything else. Through these encounters, we validate our experiences as men, lose our deep-seated dependence on women, and find the same-gender counterpart we need who truly understands what it is like to be a man.[4]

Apparently agreeing with Hicks, Rod Cooper, the National Director of Education for Promise Keepers, expresses concern that "men talk with women" as opposed to "other men about intimate things."[5]

Notice that the proposed remedy Promise Keepers latches onto is not to teach men how to be better friends to their wives, but rather, *to teach men to relate to one another like women relate to one another.* Instead of capturing this valuable opportunity to turn husbands to their wives, Promise Keepers turns men to one another. While the proposed remedy may very well undermine intimacy within the marriage relationship (addressed in chapter eight), notice how the remedy assumes that men need to get together with each other just like women so that they, like women, can work through the "issues" of life together. Geoff Gorsuch and Dan Shaffer, for example, approvingly write about two men who learned to share each other's "pain" and "discovered that the private scars that men are so hesitant to share are often the passports to each other's heart."[6] With passports like that, one is left to wonder where they are traveling.

We also read of coach McCartney who was described in the inaugural issue of *New Man* as being "like most men" because he "is emotionally challenged when it comes to sharing his soul with his wife."[7] This article, in the spirit of political correctness, simply pronounces "most men" guilty of the crime of being "emotionally challenged" without any evidence to prove the charge. The only "evidence" adduced is the unsubstantiated assumption that men don't relate to their wives as their wives relate to them. And as we have already seen, men are told by Promise Keepers that to be better husbands, they must learn to relate to other men like women relate to each other. Where did we ever get the idea that hanging out with the guys necessarily makes us better husbands? Where did we ever get the idea that unless we give other men "passports" to our hearts we cannot become the husbands that God has called us to be? And where did we get the idea that the Bible requires either?

Though Promise Keepers may deny the obvious, the model it holds before men for relating to their wives and other men is a *feminine* model. If women enjoy tea parties with one another, so should men. We call this model the tea party mentality. But is it right?

To begin with, it assumes that what works for women will work for men. Even worse, it assumes, without any biblical proof, that what *is* the case with women *should* be the case for men. Because women are comfortable getting together and chatting, Promise Keepers assumes that the same should be true for men. In this way, Promise Keepers uncritically adopts a feminine model of relationships flowing from the relationship-orientation of women, and makes that feminine model normative for men. Admittedly, men need to be more understanding with their wives by loving them, nurturing them, honoring them, cherishing them, and the like. But men are not called by God to become their wife's girlfriend. They are not called to sacrifice their masculinity on the altar of the secular "sensitive male" of the 90's which has very little, if anything, in common with true, biblical masculinity.

Who's Wearing the Pants?

Promise Keepers not only feminizes men by mandating that they relate to one another like women, but also by teaching men to become the kind of husbands their wives want them to become. But becoming the kind of husband *Sally* wants you to become may not necessarily be the kind of husband *God* wants you to become. Certainly Sally may make suggestions respectfully, but never is she to set the pace in the home. That's what it means to act as the head of the home. Headship is not a dictatorship, but it is not a democracy either.

Some Promise Keepers authors haven't caught on to this distinction. McCartney has often said that the men who attend Promise Keepers conferences "are not sent home to rule the domain but to rule alongside" their wives. While men are to lead by serving their wives, they are also called by God to rule their domain—the home. They are not to rule tyrannically, but they are to rule nonetheless. Between the sinful extremes of authoritarianism and abdication, there is biblical headship in the home.

Some Promise Keepers authors actually go so far as shunning McCartney's image of a wife alongside her husband only to put wives *ahead* of their husbands. In a *New Man* article entitled, "Daddy Time," for example, Patricia Rushford tells fathers who recognize their failure as leaders but who want to do something about it to resist asserting their authority over their wives:

> If Mom has been the primary caregiver she may resist your efforts or feel you are undermining her efforts. Resist taking control or asserting authority. Rather, talk about your concerns and desires to be a better father.[8]

The buzzword for Rushford is "control."

The ever-popular Gary Smalley joins in this chorus exalting free-wheeling wives and denouncing husbands who want to "control" them. He encourages husbands to "participate as a family instead of controlling every situation."[9] Instead of leading your wife, Smalley encourages you

> to tell her she is equally capable of calling the plays—that means not only encouraging her to have a say in running the team, but to listen to her viewpoint and try the plays she calls.[10]

As opposed to calling the shots, men are exhorted to "(l)et her call the shots without always having to explain or defend herself."[11] While husbands may delegate certain tasks to ther wives such as managing household finances, even then, husbands maintain ultimate responsibility and accountability before the Lord for such tasks.

But delegating certain tasks is not the same thing as letting wives call the shots with husbandly headship nowhere in sight. Let's imagine a scenario to see how Smalley's advice would play out. Suppose your wife is angry with you (justifiably!), and it is not a matter which love can cover either for you or for her. Suppose still further that she wants to go to bed without clearing up the situation. Suppose you lovingly seek forgiveness and say that you really should talk it out since Christians ought not to let the sun go down on their anger (Eph. 4:26). Suppose still further that she rebuffs you. Now what do you do? Do you follow Smalley's advice and let her "call the play"? Or, do you exercise your gentle, but loving, headship in the home by not allowing your wife to "fumble" into the hands of the opponent?

Which is honoring to God? Which is honoring to your wife? The answer is obvious to the rest of us, but apparently not to Smalley who writes:

> One surefire way to dishonor your wife is to impose your boundaries on her. She will flag you every single time, because she will interpret it as your being controlling . . .

. . . Whenever freedoms are restricted rather than encouraged, you dishonor her.[12]

Really? Does Christ dishonor us by imposing His boundaries on us? Isn't our freedom in Him true freedom only when it operates within the boundaries He has set forth in His Word? Aren't we Christ's bride? And aren't husbands supposed to love and lead their wives as Christ loves and leads His bride, the church (Eph. 5:22-33)? Is Christ, on Smalley's logic, "controlling"? Does Christ dishonor us?

We do not dishonor our wives when we love them as Christ loves us. In his advice on this point, we are afraid Smalley has missed the mark.

The Need of the Hour

Other examples of the feminizing tendency of Promise Keepers teaching abound. In the name of masculinity, men are urged in a Promise Keepers study guide to create a fellowship "whose ticket for admission is the admission of wounds" or to start giving "Purple Heart Awards" to men with "broken spirits."[13] Not exactly a masculine response. And New Man is filled with repeated calls for increased sensitivity: real men have feelings too, eight steps to intimacy, and so forth. Then there is Hicks, who, in The Masculine Journey, expresses a desire for wayward young men to be indulged after "their first experience with the police, or their first drunk, or their first experience with sex or drugs . . ."[14] Hicks suggests that the time be used as a teachable moment and a "rite of passage." He suggests that the "true elders could come forward and confess their own adolescent sins and congratulate the next generation for being human."[15] Whatever else this response is, it most certainly is not a biblical, masculine response. It is not strong, masculine leadership for young men at all. It is indulgence, which is the last thing such boys need.

The current wisdom permeating the Promise Keepers movement does acknowledge the need for a recovery of masculinity. But this current wisdom also assumes that men must become more like women, first to themselves, and then to others. This emphasis is whooped as true masculinity: real men cry and suffer deep pain. But actually the current wisdom is like a drunk in a bar ordering a stiff one as a preparation for his forthcoming promised sobriety. Before turning around, before converting, he thinks he must take at least three more steps in the other direction.

The need of the hour is masculine confidence; we need men with backbone. And what do we have? We have men off in the corner, moaning and whining about their childhoods, keening over long-remembered hurts, snuffling about aimlessly, and getting in touch with their own personal selves. Modern man is off looking for a mommy, and Promise Keepers is unfortunately encouraging him to keep looking. While the movement is to be commended for attacking the feminization of Christian men, it unwittingly has contributed to that very feminization. While Promise Keepers emphasizes restoring true masculinity, it at the same time encourages men to head in an effeminate direction. If the airplane is flying east, to leave the seat and head west up the aisle is an inadequate response. In the name of going westward, Promise Keepers is headed eastward, tail wind and all.

Still, Promise Keepers is *not* the problem. The movement simply represents an initial and inadequate response to a problem which was overwhelming us long before Promise Keepers ever came on the scene. That problem is one of rampant masculine abdication. The Promise Keepers movement has provided the valuable service of identifying this problem on a national level. However, Promise Keepers is still to be faulted, for while it insists that this problem be addressed with courage and integrity, it has allowed the movement to be steered by professional handlers into various forms of femininity, moral cowardice, and doctrinal compromise.

The need is certainly great. Whenever "real masculinity" prances around in a skirt and blouse, it must be attacked,
and attacked by Christians with a warm enthusiasm. The
secular doctrine of the "sensitive male" must be criticized,
wherever it appears, and soundly, with a baseball bat. Psychological and theological flimflam merchants, with all their
estrogenic supplements, must be hooted off the public stage.
If Promise Keepers were to engage the enemy with full integrity, it could have a tremendous impact for good in
Christianity's cultural war against effeminacy. But as the situation now stands, it has only played into the hands of the
enemy, and has failed to use its influence to assault effeminacy as it ought to have done.

The Sharp Edges of the Truth

This analysis may prove to be offensive to some, although
giving offense is not our intent. But even the modern resis-
tance to pointed criticism does not reflect a manly concern
for biblical obedience; it points to specimens of men who
get their feelings hurt on the sharp edges of the truth. Because we live in such an effeminate culture, especially in the
evangelical church, the temptation for proud men is to think
the only way out of their sin is to cultivate an effeminate
form of pride. This is not sanctification. It amounts to castration. Because the fundamental antithesis in our fallen
world is covenantal and ethical, not gender-related, ungodly
men must become godly men. Ungodly women must become godly women. Men who seek to get away from arrogance and pride by becoming more like their wives have
misplaced this antithesis. And so when a brother comes alongside with an admonition, the appropriate response is not to
take offense. Faithful are the wounds of a friend.

Christian men must be called to true confidence. And
this masculine and biblical confidence avoids the sin of *hu-*

bris without falling into the common error of confusing humility and effeminacy. The word *confidence* comes from the Latin, meaning *with faith*. A man who walks in faith may certainly be accused of being arrogant and proud, but such accusations are simply the cost of doing business. And the restoration of biblical masculinity is business that must be done, and done immediately by all Christian men.

By insisting that men relate to one another like women and that men need to become the kind of men their wives want them to become, the Promise Keepers movement, in the name of making men more masculine, has actually made them more feminine.

The Promise Keepers movement is in deep tension with itself. It doesn't want a church full of sissies, but then turns around and encourages men to become a bunch of cry babies. It wants men to lead the home, but then wants them to follow the lead of their wives. Perhaps this tension is what led one astute reporter to conclude that Promise Keepers, as reflected in the typical conference, is "both a reaction against feminism and an accommodation to it."[16]

Well said.

---

[1] *SPPK*, p. 73.

[2] *The Awesome Power of Shared Beliefs*, (Dallas, TX: Word Publishing), 1995, p. 11 (hereafter "*TAPSB*").

[3] Chip MacGregor, "Why Do I Need a Mentor?" *New Man*, January/February, 1995, vol. 2, no. 1, p. 69.

[4] Robert Hicks, *What Makes a Man?* (Colorado Springs, CO: Navpress, 1992), p. 137 (hereafter "*WMAM*").

[5] Rod Cooper, "Into Me See," *New Man*, March/April, 1995, vol. 2, no. 2, p. 42.

[6] Geoff Gorsuch and Dan Shaffer, *Brothers!* (Colorado Springs, CO: Navpress, 1994), p. 79.

[7] David Halbrook, "The Real Coach McCartney," *New Man*, July/August 1994, vol. 1, no. 1, p. 30.

[8] Patricia H. Rushford, July/August, 1995, vol. 2, no. 4, p. 93.

[9] Gary Smalley, "Treat Her Like a Queen," *New Man*, January/February, 1996, vol. 3, no. 1, p. 33, quoting anonymous source.

[10] *Ibid.*, p. 30.

[11] *Ibid.*, p. 32.

[12] *Ibid.*, p. 33.

[13] *The Masculine Journey Study Guide* (Colorado Springs, CO: Navpress, 1993), pp. 52, 57-58 (hereafter, "*TMJSG*").

[14] *Ibid.*, p. 177.

[15] *Ibid.*

[16] Joseph P. Shapiro, "Heavenly Promises," *U.S. News & World Report*, October 2, 1995, p. 70.

❈ FOUR ❈

Back to Eden

Christian men are called to true, biblical confidence. And, as we have noted before, for that confidence to be truly biblical, it must be truly covenantal. Promise Keepers instinctively recognizes the need to call men to true, covenantal masculinity. Commendably, some speakers and writers have addressed the importance of covenants for men of God. Even the Maranatha! Promise Band cut a special song for Promise Keepers entitled "Godly Men," which speaks explicitly of promise keepers entering into covenant with God:

> And as we enter in this covenant
> We will seek Your holy face
> To become men of integrity
> Perfected by Your grace
>
> Lord as we enter in
> We pledge to live
> As godly men
>
> Lord help us turn from sin
> And begin again
> As godly men[1]

While "Godly Men" deserves high marks for helping men see their need to "turn from sin and begin again as godly men," it nevertheless reveals a profound misunderstanding of how it is that we are to turn from sin and begin again. This misunderstanding stems from the notion that by making the now-famous seven promises, we somehow "enter into covenant" with God, which then serves as the basis for repentance and growth in godliness.

Without a doubt, covenant masculinity, biblically understood, involves repentance and growth in godliness. But the basis for that repentance and growth in godliness is not a covenant of works based upon what *we* have done or promised, but rather, a covenant of grace based only upon what *Christ* has done for us already, since in Him all the promises of God find their "yes" (2 Cor. 1:20).

Covenants Then and Now

To see why our works or promises never become the basis of relating to God covenantally, we must first understand what covenants are all about. And, in order to do that, we must recognize that covenants are rooted in the very character of God Himself. God always deals with men by means of covenants because He is a covenant-making and covenant-keeping God. This sounds nice, and very religious, but what does it *mean*?

Covenants between God and His people are solemn bonds, sovereignly administered, with attendant blessings and curses. Hence, the term "covenant" describes the way God deals with us as His people and our seed. He promises to be our God and to make us, in turn, His people.

At the dawn of creation, God entered into covenant with Adam, as the covenant head or representative of the entire human race (Hos. 6:7; Rom. 5:12-19). In this covenant, which is sometimes called *the covenant of works*, God promised Adam, as the covenant head or representative of the entire human race, eternal life on the condition that he obey the specific command as well as the creation ordinances entrusted to him in the Garden. Sadly, Adam rebelled against that sovereign and gracious covenant and brought upon himself and all his posterity the curse of the covenant: sin, misery, and death.

In pronouncing His divine judgment on the principal actors in the divine and human drama which we now call the Fall, God imposed a fundamental antithesis in human history between the seed of the woman (God's people) and the seed of the serpent (God's enemies). But at the same time, God also established a second and more glorious covenant, known as *the covenant of grace*. This covenant was established when God declared to the serpent, "And I will put enmity between you and the woman, and between your seed and her seed; He shall bruise you on the head, and you shall bruise him on the heel" (Gen. 3:15).

Thus, at one of the bleakest moments of human history, God not only imposed an antithesis between the seed of the woman and the seed of the serpent in history that would extend into eternity, He also continued to display His marvelous grace. Although the seed of the woman would be at war with the seed of the serpent from that point forward, God promised to redeem the seed of the woman through one of her descendants, who would decisively and eternally crush the head of the serpent.

From that point on, God unfolded and expanded this marvelous covenant of grace through Noah (Gen. 6:17-22; 8:20-22; 9:1-7; 9:8-17), Abraham (Gen. 15-17), Moses (Ex. 2:24), and David (2 Sam. 7:12-16), anticipating the seed of the woman to come. Then, in the fullness of time, the anticipation declared in the Garden pointed to the manger, the cross, and eventually, the empty tomb. Christ, the seed of the woman, crushed the serpent and continues to do so by ransoming His people from their slavery to sin, uniting them in marriage as His bride, avenging them against the seed of the serpent, and regaining their lost inheritance. He continues to work on our behalf and has also promised us that the gates of Hell will not prevail against us (Matt. 16:18). Not only will He be our God and the God of our seed after us, but we shall be His people, both now and forever.

From a biblical point of view, there are only two covenants the Lord has established with His people. This means there are only two ways of relating to God. One is the covenant of works (based on man's perfect works), and the other is the covenant of grace (based on grace through faith on account of Christ's perfect work for us). Since Adam broke the covenant of works, man no longer can relate to God by means of his works. He may try to do so, but such efforts are doomed to failure. For even assuming the impossible—that a man were never to sin against God—he would still bear the guilt, corruption, and pollution he inherited because of Adam's sin. It is because we are sinners by nature through Adam that we sin each day. Even though the Bible clearly tells us that we are sinners by nature and by conduct, some still think that they can relate to God by means of their works. But no matter what they think, their works will never commend them to God. As Paul succinctly stated,

> For as many as are of the works of the Law are under a curse; for it is written, "Cursed is every one who does not abide by all things written in the book of the law, to perform them" (Gal. 2:10; Deut. 27:26).

Yet we know that we do not perform all the works of the law, for Paul has taught us elsewhere that "all have sinned and fall short of the glory of God" (Rom. 3:23). Thus, our works cannot be the covenantal basis of how we relate to God.

From start to finish, we relate to God on the basis of His grace. God graciously draws us into a covenant with Him, graciously enables us to repent, graciously forgives us, and graciously enables us to walk in obedience to Him as we grow in godliness.

Unable to relate to God on the basis of the covenant of works, we have become His people and relate to Him only on the basis of the covenant of grace. Whereas the covenant of works was made between the Father representing the trinity and Adam as the representative of all His descendants, the covenant of grace was made between the Father and Christ as the representative of His people. Whereas Adam failed to do what he was required to do by the covenant of works, Christ perfectly fulfilled in the covenant of grace. Whereas Adam plunged himself and all his descendants into sin and death in the covenant of works, Christ exalted His descendants by bestowing upon them righteousness and life in the covenant of grace. Christ, the "last Adam," undid what the first Adam did and did what the first Adam failed to do (Rom. 5:12-19).

Hence, the conditions of the covenant of grace need no human supplement; they have been fulfilled perfectly by Christ. We are not covenantally related to God based on what we do or what we promise. Rather, we are covenantally related to God based upon what Christ graciously has done and the promises He has made and fulfilled for us already. By reverting back to the covenant of works in Eden as the basis for relating to God, the Promise Keepers movement has misunderstood the covenant of grace between God and His people. When we use the phrase "Promise Keepers" we must understand the nature of the promise—and who made it. Again, Christ is our only hope for He alone is the only Promise Keeper.

As Goes the Family . . .

Just as God deals with mankind through covenants, so He created us in such a way that we also must deal with one another under Him by means of covenants. At the center of our lives we find that such covenants are inescapable; we cannot function apart from them because they are built into our bones. The covenants in this category are those of marriage/family (Mal. 3:14-15), the church (Luke 22:20), and the civil order (Rom. 13:1-7).

These three covenant institutions have been established among us directly by the hand of God. We have no authority to alter or abolish them to suit our tastes or desires. But it is not enough for Christians to acknowledge the existence of these covenants. We must also correctly understand their relationship to one another. It would be a serious mistake to line them up in a row of three, and then simply assign respective biblical duties to each. Each covenant institution certainly does have its respective duties, but we must first understand that the covenantal institutions of the church and the civil order are made up of family units. Each family has certain assigned duties within its own sphere: education, health care, provision of food, and all the rest. But together, families also contribute a molecular strength in the makeup of the two other trans-family governments—the church and the civil order. That is, each family makes this contribution for blessing when it is offered in understanding belief, and it is received by the two broader covenant communities with the same believing mind.

Because of the crisis of masculinity in the home, that representation is not being offered by our households, and if it were offered, it would be received by our civil order only with laughter, and by our churches with an ignorant theological indignation. In short, we all, from top to bottom, are in high rebellion against God's design for family and culture. We in the church like to disguise that rebellion by talking about "family values" which amounts, as far as we can tell, to a vibrant desire for more G-rated movies. But we never talk about familial representation in the church, or familial authority in the civil realm.

This breakdown is the result of men becoming spiritual eunuchs. At the heart of each family is a man. He cannot help being biologically male, but disobedience can certainly turn him away from being truly masculine; that is, a truly masculine man embraces headship, takes the initiative, serves responsibly, provides for his own, and represents his household to the other governments established by God. The question is not *whether* man is head of the house; the question is *what kind* of head he *is* and *what kind* of head he *should, by God's grace, become.*

Modern Christian men who abdicate their call to covenant headship can be divided into two categories: those who have acquiesced to the current dictates requiring effeminacy, and those who think they have not acquiesced because they are still allowed to beat their chests at home. Those in the former category need to renounce their effeminacy and seek, by God's grace, to become true men. Those in the latter category must come to realize their broader cultural impotence. What does your leadership in the household mean? That you get to hold the remote when the family watches television? That you get to park the car when the family goes to church? What it really means is that you have the responsibility before God to wake up.

The Abortion of the Family

As just one example of the wholesale abdication of true masculinity by Christian men and the resulting lethargy it entails, consider our reaction to the Supreme Court's infamous decision to allow the slaughter of infants. The Christians of our nation were so covenantally blind that we did not see that this infamous ruling was not only the abortion of untold millions of infants but also the abortion of the biblical family. This is not to minimize in any way the horrific nature of the abortion carnage; God is just and He will judge. But why didn't we even see the other implication of the Court's decision? When a woman is considering an abortion, the Court held that this decision is to be made between her and her doctor. As far as our civil order is concerned, whether the woman is married or not is completely irrelevant. The fact that a man has taken a solemn vow assuming covenantal responsibility for his offspring was judged by our highest Court to be a matter of *no legal consequence*. It was decreed to be superfluous.

It is difficult to understand what is more tragic, the decision of the Court to permit the slaughter of children, or the decision of the Court to slaughter the Christian family and the subsequent inability of modern Christians even to notice that the Court declared every child in the nation to be illegitimate. While the nation laughed at the prime time cartoon "Wait Till Your Father Gets Home," the Supreme Court sent him packing once for all.

With the abortion decision, the rejection of the legal reality of family covenants finally came to the shedding of blood. But this lawlessness had been at work in our civil order for well over a century. We did not notice that our children had been declared illegitimate because we had already believed the lie of individualism fostered by a pagan revolution on another continent. When a nation no longer receives the ambassadors of another nation, it is in effect refusing to recognize that nation. When the civil order and the church refuse to receive the divinely-appointed representative head of the household, the same conclusion is unavoidable. The embassy was closed and boarded up for good measure.

In this respect the churches of our nation have been just as guilty as our civil establishment. A family church is thought to be one with lots of kids present and an efficient nursery. But in most churches, officially speaking, the nurseries are full of aliens. How many churches reckon membership by household? How many churches vote by household, with the head of each house representing that family? How many churches even encourage families to worship God together as families, from the oldest to the youngest?

Headed in the Wrong Direction

We have forgotten the meaning of true, biblical masculinity. We have turned away from the principle which ties all covenants together, whether divine or human. Remember, a covenant is a solemn bond, sovereignly administered, with attendant blessings and curses. Every covenant home needs a head, both to oversee the home and to represent the home to other covenant entities.

Willingness to embrace that responsibility at the level of each household is biblical masculinity. Refusal to do so at the level of each household is covenantal castration. We must mark it well; abdication does not remove the covenant responsibilities as far as God is concerned. What it does is bring down tumbling cultural curses like an earthslide. And here we are, with rulers who do not see any liberty in the law of God. "Why do they not see?" we wonder. But we are the ones who are blind to the covenant and cannot see that such rulers are God's judgment on *us*.

Exhorted by somebody to "get involved," we think the solution is to "throw the bums out." But the "bums" are simply the hand of the Lord upon us. The only way out is repentance. The only safe way to flee from the wrath of the Lord is to turn to Him. The Lord says, " I will give children to be their princes, and babes shall rule over them. The people will be oppressed, every one by another and every one by his neighbor; the child will be insolent toward the elder, and the base toward the honorable" (Is. 3:4-5). The Lord is angry with us, and we see results on every hand. "As for My people, children are their oppressors, and women rule over them. O My people! Those who lead you cause you to err, and destroy the way of your paths" (Is. 3:12). And as a people, we do not yet see the causes of His just judgment upon us.

Repentance must begin in each household, with husbands and fathers turning from their effeminacy. Tragically, much of our current folly is effeminacy in the name of Christ.

Contrary to popular teaching on the subject, a man's duty is not to be a really sweet guy, well-liked by all at church. Much of the effort being expended on masculine renewal today is nothing more than a discipleship program for kinder, gentler men, a pale copy of the secular men's movement of a few years back.

Tragically, for all its talk about promises and covenants, Promise Keepers has not yet grasped the implications of true covenantal masculinity in the home, the church, and the civil order. In fact, instead of recognizing the home, church, and civil order as covenantal institutions and encouraging men, by God's grace, to begin to exercise true masculinity in each institution, Promise Keepers wastes all kinds of time manufacturing a fourth covenantal institution unknown in Scripture: the independent men's small group (the flaws of which we address in more detail in chapter 10). Then, not content to stop at creating an extra-biblical covenantal institution, Promise Keepers also has manufactured a plethora of additional covenants to operate within those extra-biblical covenantal institutions:

1. The Covenant of Affirmation: "I will love you and affirm you no matter what you have said or done. I love you as you are for what Christ wants to make of you."

2. The Covenant of Availability: "Anything I have—time, energy, and resources—are all at your disposal. I give these to the group in a unique way."

3. The Covenant of Regularity: "I will give a regular part of my time to this group when it decides to meet. I will give that time priority on my schedule."

4. The Covenant of Prayer: "I promise to pray for you, to uphold you, and to attempt to be sensitive to the Holy Spirit concerning your needs."

5. The Covenant of Openness: "I will let you know who I am and where I am as a person in my hopes and hurts. I will need you!"

6. The Covenant of Honesty: "I will be honest in my feedback to you in what I sense and feel coming from you."

7. The Covenant of Confidentiality: "What goes on in this group stays here. I will say nothing that may be traced back to my covenant partners."

8. The Covenant of Accountability: "You have the right to expect growth from me so that you may benefit from my gifts as I do yours. You have a right to ask me questions in that regard."[2]

While future chapters will explore whether these kinds of covenants are truly biblical, the far more important point shouldn't be missed for the time being: Promise Keepers has created a fourth covenantal institution out of thin air which, at times, competes with, rivals, and subtly undermines the covenantal institutions God already *has* created: the family, the church, and the civil order. The pseudo-covenantal institution of the men's small group is an unnecessary intrusion into the covenant order created by God. It is simply another form of effeminacy parading in disguise, with a whole lot of covenantalese to hide that fact.

In contrast to this pseudo-covenantal masculinity so popular today, true covenantal masculinity causes those who embrace it to assume a mantle of strength, and the demeanor of masculine leadership first in the home. And when men have assumed godly responsibility within the home, they must then bring that representative headship to bear outside the home in the church and the civil order. This is the real test. A man who thinks he leads at home, but who has a failure of nerve as the family's ambassador outside the home will have no more cultural impact than the average bossy college roommate.

The necessary repentance can spread first to the church, as it is given an opportunity to receive, for the first time in generations, the heads of covenant households in their official representative capacity. As the church is reformed in this way, it will have its former and long-forgotten strength restored. And then a biblical pattern will finally be displayed that may be safely imitated in the civil realm. But until then, all attempts at cultural reform are sweeping water uphill.

Through it all, we have the Lord's blessed covenantal challenge and assurance: "Who is the man that fears the LORD? Him shall He teach in the way He chooses. He himself shall dwell in prosperity, And his descendants shall inherit the earth. The secret of the LORD is with those who fear Him, And He will show them His covenant." (Ps. 25:13,14). Do we really fear Him? He is the Lord of the family, the Lord of the church, and the Lord of the civil order who, by His grace, has called us into the covenant of grace with Him and has promised to bless us as we, by His grace, learn to fear Him in all we do. May He be pleased to grant to us the great reformation of true covenant renewal. May He have mercy!

---

[1] Scott Wesley Brown and David Hampton, "Godly Men," *Raise the Standard, Promise Keepers Conference Edition for 1995* (Laguna Hills, CA: Maranatha! Music, 1995).

[2] *Brothers!*, pp. 50-51.

❄ FIVE ❄

The Tower of Psychobabble

After the Fall and the degradation that flowed from it, the inhabitants of the earth fell prey to just another "good" idea—to make a name for themselves by constructing a tower that would reach to the heavens. Presumptuously, they thought that they could bring the Infinite down to the finite or perhaps more accurately, that the finite, with stone and mortar, could reach the Infinite. So they got out their mallets and started pounding. Humorous? Not really, or at least not to God, who judged them severely for their foolishness, and ended up scattering them and confusing their languages (Gen. 11:1-9).

No doubt the Tower of Babel, as their edifice came to be called, ultimately points us to Christ. For it teaches us that instead of man making a name for himself by erecting a tower to try to reach the heavens, only to end up humiliated and confused in tongue, God descended from heaven as a man who spoke our tongue and led those "of every tribe and tongue and nation" heavenward as He was exalted and bestowed with the name that is above very name.

Nevertheless, the Tower of Babel also serves as a helpful illustration of the futility of would-be human efforts to reach or rival God. Yet that is exactly what the psychologized gospel of the late-twentieth century has done: it has tried to reach God by shaping and molding human behavior—by human effort. We call this new attempt to reach the heavens by human effort the Tower of Psychobabble.

Though Promise Keepers was not the principal architect of the Tower of Psychobabble, it has, from its inception, joined itself to the construction crew. While Promise Keepers is not *the* problem, it has become part of the problem by helping to heap stone upon stone as the Tower makes its way heavenward.

Dishing It Up

To be sure, some Promise Keepers authors and speakers have had enough theological acumen to sense that the construction crew may not be building a truly heavenly edifice. But even after offering the insight, they still unwittingly contribute to the overall effort. Robert Liparulo, for example, noted in *New Man* that "secular psychology often clashes with biblical teachings,"[1] but then, in the same breath, he recommends a book that psychologizes the book of Romans away. For example, Paul's struggle with surviving sin in Romans 7 was really "a warfare against compulsive behavior, waged entirely within the flesh or the old nature."[2]

In the same issue of *New Man*, evangelist and pastor, Greg Laurie, wrote an article entitled "Mr. Nice God," in which he correctly observed that "(t)he books selling in Christian bookstores today are the 'touchy feely' ones that focus on self-esteem, self-fulfillment, and self-analysis, while devotionals and missionary biographies gather dust on the shelves."[3] Laurie then approvingly quotes an article from *Newsweek* which insightfully criticizes the myopic, self-absorbed "religion" of baby boomers:

> Unlike earlier religious revivals, the aim this time is support, not salvation; help rather than holiness; a circle of spiritual equals rather than an authoritative church or guide.

A group affirmation of self is at the top of the agenda, which is why some of the least demanding churches are now in the greatest demand.[4]

Again, Laurie is right on target when he quotes a cover story on spirituality in *U.S. News & World Report,* which noted:

American religion has taken on the aura of pop psychology. Many congregations have multiplied their membership by going light on theology and offering worshippers a steady diet of sermons and support groups that emphasize personal fulfillment.[5]

But then, amazingly, Laurie follows Liparulo's lead by taking back with one hand what he has given with the other. After quoting *Newsweek* and *U.S. News* with apparent approval, he turns around and gives a foothold to pop psychology in the church:

While it isn't wrong to address issues like these, it is a grave error to make them the central focus of ministry . . . Why is there not more emphasis on God's attributes of holiness, righteousness and hatred for sin?[6]

According to Laurie, a *little* pop psychology of personal fulfillment is acceptable as long as it is not a "central focus." In other words, we can pamper congregations by feeding them the pablum of pop psychology as an appetizer, just as long as we don't serve it up as the main course. Laurie should know better. And he shouldn't be surprised at the nauseating results.

When we cater to the offerings of pop psychology which starts from the premise that "I'm okay, you're okay"—that man is basically good—we will never get around to "God's attributes of holiness, righteousness and hatred for sin." Those doctrines have been marginalized from the getgo. They have been rendered irrelevant and meaningless by the very pop psychology Laurie wants to make room for. We have filled our bellies with so much of the appetizer that we no longer have any room for the main course.

The Great Compromise

What Laurie does not grasp, William Kilpatrick, an educational psychologist at Boston College, has had no problem grasping. In *The Emperor's New Clothes: The Naked Truth about the New Psychology,* Kilpatrick sizes up the danger of blending Christianity and psychology. He writes that Christianity's assimilation of modern psychology represents

> a case of a confused and conciliatory Christianity willing to lop off limbs from the Body of Christ in order to fit it to a procrustean bed of psychology. Although there is room for some accommodation between Christianity and psychology, there are some areas where it is clearly a matter of either/or. Either the psychologist is right or the Christian is right. Both can't be.
>
> In such cases, attempts to reconcile Christianity to psychology will actually have the effect of undermining the Christian point of view.[7]

Like it or not, the true gospel and pop psychology cannot cohabit without some compromise and without eventually conceiving and giving birth to the illegitimate child of the psychologized gospel. That child has grown and is running amok in the church today.

Esteeming Ourselves Highly

Kilpatrick goes on to note that the "most obvious example" of psychology undermining the Christian worldview is the notion of self-esteem.[8] Oblivious to this fact, Promise Keepers speakers and writers have told us that our basic problem as men is that our self-esteem is too low, that we just need to feel better about ourselves. We are told, for example, that we should not procrastinate because "(s)tudies reveal that procrastination destroys both productivity and self-esteem."[9] So what are you waiting for? Gary Smalley and John Trent, for example, tell us in the first official book released by Promise Keepers, that

> The degree of self-control you have in your life is in direct proportion to the degree of acceptance you have for yourself. Put another way, if you don't value yourself, you won't "pull in the reins" on actions and attitudes that will affect you for the worse.[10]

They proceed to tell us that the failure to pull in the reins lies at the heart of any addiction. Putting it all together, Smalley and Trent have told us that someone who doesn't "accept" himself enough (read: have enough self-esteem) will not pull in the reins and will end up with an addiction. By implication, then, a lack of self-esteem is the root of addiction. If we dare call addiction what it usually is—sin—Smalley and Trent have just "proven" that a lack of self-esteem is the root of at least some sin.

And if we have accurately represented the Promise Keepers view of the connection between self-esteem and sin, then we would expect the Promise Keepers to teach that Christ, at least in part, came to save us from our low sense of self-esteem. And that is exactly what we find. In the very same book, Promise Keepers founder, Bill McCartney, frankly admits how he wanted to give his life to Christ in order to "gain some real satisfaction" since he "wasn't feeling good" about himself.[11] A few pages later in the same book, William Gaultiere argues that if we as men struggle with "guilt, pride, or apathy," we "probably have a distorted image of God" fueled by our imperfect fathers here on earth.[12] He then takes us to the parable of the prodigal son as a feel-good story and concludes by noting:

> We men who struggle with guilt, pride, or apathy are prodigal sons. The father is God. We need to experience the same kind of fatherly love and forgiveness *in order to feel better about ourselves as men.*[13]

Notice that according to Gaultiere, not only do *we* need God's forgiveness in order to feel better about ourselves, but *God* Himself feels pretty good about us, too. Yet another Promise Keepers author, Rod Cooper, expressed some of the same sentiments when he confidently asks, "What is so valuable about us that God would send His only son?"[14] To bolster his point, he then quotes Psalm 8:4 ("What is man that thou art mindful of him?") and concludes by writing, "(a)pparently, God sees something in us that we too often fail to see in each other."[15] With this assessment, Robert Hicks concurs by writing that "there is something to be valued and esteemed in the self of every human being."[16]

Enough already! The whole point of the gospel is that, apart from Christ, God found *nothing* good in us, and that apart from Him, we have nothing to offer Him. All of our supposed righteousness is as "filthy rags" in His sight (Is. 64:6). There is "no one who is righteous, not even one" (Rom. 3:10). There is "no one who does good, there is not even one" (v. 12). "All we like sheep have gone astray" (Is. 53:6). We "were by nature children of wrath" (Eph. 2:3), "sons of disobedience" (v. 2), "dead in our trespasses and sins" (v. 1).

So just what is there to feel good about, anyway? The biblical answer is that "no one is good but God alone" (Mk. 10:18). We have nothing to feel good about *in ourselves* but we do have everything to feel good about *in Christ.* For though we had sinned and rebelled against Him and though we deserve nothing but His utmost wrath and condemnation, He, "being rich in mercy" toward us, "even when we were dead in our transgressions, made us alive together with

Christ (by grace you have been saved), and raised us up with Him in the heavenly places, in Christ Jesus" (Eph. 2:4-6).

According to Paul, our goodness is nowhere in sight. Just to drive home the point, he adds only two verses later: "For by grace you have been saved through faith; and that *not of yourselves*, it is the gift of God; *not as a result of works, that no one should boast*" (v. 8, emphasis added).

Salvation is by grace. It is a gift of God, not a reward for who you are or what you have done. But the good news of the gospel can never be the good news unless we first receive the bad news about ourselves. We not only lacked the good God required of us, we were positively evil. The problem of the natural man is not that he fails to esteem or love himself enough; it is that he loves himself too much. That's the bad news. But the good news is that Christ's love goes forth conquering and to conquer. He lived the life of perfect righteousness that we failed to live, and He died in our place for our sin. In the words of Paul, God "made Him who knew no sin to be sin on our behalf, that we might become the righteousness of God in Him" (2 Cor. 5:21).

The good news is not in us. In fact, it has nothing to do with us or how we esteem ourselves. The good news is in Christ and how we are esteemed in Him! It was not our goodness, but His, that saved us. It is not our goodness, but His, that commends us to God, even now. It will not be our goodness, but His, that will result in our yet future glorification. Everything we have in the Christian life we have in Him (Eph. 1:3).

This is the gospel Paul preached and jealously guarded. So adamant was he about this that, under the inspiration of the Holy Spirit, he pronounced anathemas on anyone who preached any other "gospel," which, as he put it, is really not another, for there can be but one true gospel (Gal.1:6-9).

Many counterfeits. One original. What currency is the Promise Keepers trading in? By psychologizing away the gospel, Promise Keepers is shortchanging itself and the body

of Christ. As Kilpatrick so poignantly put it long before
Promise Keepers ever came on the scene, when we embrace
psychology's concept of self-esteem, we reduce the cross of
Christ to a meaningless gesture:

> (T)he psychological perspective [of self-esteem] reduces the
> good news of the gospel to the status of "nice news"—"nice"
> because there was never any bad news in the first place. If
> psychology's great optimism about raw human nature is
> correct, then Christianity is not necessary: Christ's redemp-
> tive action on the cross becomes superfluous. After all, why
> should He have suffered and died to redeem us if there was
> nothing wrong with us? If all we need do to find whole-
> ness is just be ourselves, then His death sums up to a mean-
> ingless gesture, a noble but unneeded self-sacrifice.[17]

We have come full circle. Laurie began by expressing
concern about the "Mr. Nice God" many contemporary
evangelicals worship. But by making allowance for the gospel of self-esteem, he and the Promise Keepers are the very
ones who have reduced the good news of the gospel to "nice
news." *They* have portrayed the God of Holy Scripture as
"Mr. Nice God."

The Tower and the Steeple

While many Promise Keepers authors speak of our need
to be "affirmed" and to develop "self-esteem," one writer
actually went so far as applying the concept of self-esteem to
the first church he pastored, claiming "(t)hat little church
had no self-esteem."[18]

His assessment would be humorous were it not for the
fact that it reveals not only a deficient view of the gospel,
but also a deficient view of the church. Though we will spend
some time in chapter 13 describing how Promise Keepers,
notwithstanding its outward commitment to supporting the

local church, actually ends up subtly undermining it, we pause here to note briefly a few ways that Promise Keepers promotes psychobabble in the church.

The small groups fostered by Promise Keepers are fertile ground for psychobabble. See what two members of one such group had to say as they described their own experience in *The Lookout*:

> The first several weeks we met, we shared our pasts, our struggles, and what we wanted the others to hold us accountable for. After that, we started using the book, *Seven Promises of a Promise Keeper* as a guide for our meetings. We also used *Serendipity's Men: Six Sessions for Starting a Men's Group.* We are just starting into *Men Facing Temptation*, in the "Created Male and Female Bible Studies" series from InterVarsity Press.

> One of the best things we have decided to do is to affirm one person in the group at each meeting. Every week for nine weeks we chose one guy, and the rest of us would tell him why we admire him, tell him what his strengths and gifts are, and encourage him to keep his promises. The man of the week is not allowed to say anything while he is being affirmed. This exercise has helped us learn more about ourselves, gain confidence, and grow closer to one another.[19]

With friends like that . . . .

What is so unfortunate is the psychologically-steeped material these men chose to use in their "Bible" studies and the need for "affirmation" it spawned. At least they had not yet latched onto one official Promise Keepers study guide, *The Masculine Journey Study Guide*, that stops at nothing to shock the conscience. It even promotes fetishism. (NB: Readers with weak stomachs move on to the next section.) In this study guide, which is emblazoned with the official Promise Keepers logo, men are actually encouraged to get to know each other in their small group by playing "people bingo," a game requiring its participants to match as many men as possible to a grid containing various characteristics. While some of these characteristics are completely innocuous (*e.g.*, whether the respondent "plays golf or tennis competitively," or "has coached his son's soccer or baseball team," *etc.*), others are quite appalling. Those who play the game are actually supposed to go around asking more intimate questions such as whether the respondent *"is wearing boxer shorts or bikini briefs"* and whether he *"has had circumcision, vasectomy or prostate operation."*[20]

Later, this same study guide tries to get men to open up to even more intimate subjects. (NB: Again, weak readers beware!) Noting that our culture has presented initiation rites associated with the male phallus, Hicks and Gruen encourage men in the study group to discuss the following questions:

> Our culture has presented many initiation rites, or passages to manhood, that are associated with the phallus. Which ones have you experienced? Do you have a story to share with other men about one such event?
>
> • When I was potty trained and stopped wetting my bed
> • Pubic hair and growth
> • An unfortunate experience with pornography
> • My first dating experience
> • My first really embarrassing moment with a girl
> • The wedding night
> • Conceiving my first child
> • Other:[21]

After encouraging men to share stories about anatomy, pornography, and sexual intercourse with their wives, the authors then bemoan the fact that the church does not have alternative initiation rites and ask for suggestions in this regard:

> If only the church had alternative initiation rites to the

ones offered above. What creative alternative celebrations can you think of?[22]

Did Christ ever entrust His disciples with the task of creating alternative initiation rites celebrating the male phallus? Should we ever have the kinds of discussions Promise Keepers promotes, let alone in a supposed Bible study with other men in the church? Should we ever *discuss* some of these topics, much less with anyone other than our wives? What would our wives say if they really knew that we had such discussions about them with the guys? Can't these kinds of discussions incite or inflame the typical man to lust? Can these questions have any legitimate bearing on a men's Bible study group or do they simply reflect the fact that Promise Keepers, from its inception, has compromised with another gospel? Can any Promise Keepers spokesman really defend such coarse jesting, silly talk, and idle words (Eph. 5:4; Matt. 12:36-37)? If so, we would encourage him to step up to the microphone.

The same study guide not only foists neo-Freudian and neo-Jungian psychology on the church unawares, it also foists what some have seen as unbiblical encounter group theory. Professional Christian counselor, Sarah H. Leslie, has criticized *The Masculine Journey Study Guide* for promoting what she claims is an eight-week encounter group session with the artificial flavoring of biblical support.[23] According to Leslie, the study guide uncritically adopts the encounter group model which was largely discredited by the psychological community but popularized in the decade-after-vogue-would-be-evangelical community.

Each of the sessions in *The Masculine Journey Study Guide* begins by attempting to break down private inhibitions to promote group discussion, without any concept of absolute right and wrong. Says Leslie:

> The encounter group is a semi-structured group that falls within the psychological realm for the purpose of "getting

in touch with one's feelings." Encounter groups are short-term, intensive sessions, usually managed by trained leaders, which consist of exercises designed to explore and unmask inner feelings. . . The encounter group setting is supposed to provide a totally non-judgmental environment, where the individual would be accepted as he or she is, regardless of their background or psychological "baggage." In this contrived environment, experience is elevated above all else, and moral absolutes are perceived as a hindrance to growth.[24]

She goes on to note the connection between encounter groups, Serendipity Workshops, and Promise Keepers:

Unfortunately, Promise Keepers has revived the faulty encounter group structure in the Hicks study guide. The men are put through various recognizable encounter group stages that strongly resemble the "Serendipity Workshops" that were popularized by Lyman Coleman during the 1970's and 80's, which were a "Christianized" version of encounter groups mixed with some Bible study.[25]

Leslie then proves how *The Masculine Journey Study Guide* follows the same format as the Serendipity Workshops and concludes that:

the study leads men through potentially intensive, emotional turmoil and abandons them at the doorstep of rituals and ceremonies that mimic pagan religions and bear little or no resemblance to the Christian faith.[26]

Promise Keepers has also treated the church to neo-existentialist psychology in yet another study guide. We are told by Geoff Gorsuch and Dan Schaffer in *Brothers!* that "(c)onflict is good in that it forces us to leave our comfort zones and move toward authenticity."[27] Is the point of conflict in the body of Christ to lead to existential *angst* as a means of authenticating its participants? Where conflict unfortunately surfaces, it doesn't authenticate us; it gives us an opportunity to discover the truth of the Scriptures. If Bill and Fred are about to come to blows over some biblical topic, we do not rejoice that they are about to authenticate themselves. We teach them that they need to handle their disagreements biblically. Then, we take their underlying disagreement to the Bible itself to see who is right and who is wrong. Their disagreement may be a matter of indifference (whether we can drink coffee) or it may be quite significant (whether we can get drunk). But rest assured that Scripture has answers to both issues. It never leaves us in the dark.

Psychobabble and the Bible

Promise Keepers author, Robert Hicks, explicitly claims in *The Masculine Journey* that on the topic of woundedness, "both the biblical material and the contemporary literature [secular men's movement literature] are amazingly close."[28] With discernment like that once at the forefront of the Promise Keepers movement, we probably shouldn't be all too surprised when we see Promise Keepers authors "finding" their pet psychological theories in the Bible itself. Although others appear elsewhere in this book, consider these lost gems found just in the first two books Promise Keepers officially joint-ventured with Navpress:

• *Christ healed on the Sabbath, threw out the money changers from the temple, and cast out demons, all to teach us a valuable lesson in assertiveness*: "When you look at the person of Christ, you're looking at assertiveness. He healed on the Sabbath day, even when the religious leaders stood in His face and dared Him to do so. He cast money-changers from the temple and tossed verbal bombshells at the Pharisees that exploded the wall of hypocrisy surrounding them. He chased away demons and faced up to the prince of darkness.

In all these situations He relied on the healthy assertion of His power."[29] So go and do likewise!

• *God the Son demonstrated healthy dependence upon God the Father and God the Spirit but without being "co-dependent" on them*: "Even His daily dependence on the Father and the Holy Spirit wasn't an unhealthy 'co-dependence' that blurred who He was, but a strengthening interdependence of Three-in-One."[30] Perhaps a new committee should begin revising the Nicene Creed to say that Christ was "very God of very God who, without being co-dependent on the Father or the Spirit, was healthily interdependent upon them . . . ."

• *The book of Psalms is nothing more than the sound and the fury of the mentally imbalanced David*: "(T)he psalms of David [are] the musings of a manic-depressive! David's psalms are either all praise or all depression."[31]

• *Job hated God*: Job is described as "wanting to believe in a benevolent God and hating God for allowing such injustice to befall him."[32]

• *Jacob came from a dysfunctional family and wrestled God out of insecurity*: "Jacob illustrates a young man having been severely wounded by a dysfunctional family system."[33] Jacob "is so insecure in his standing with God and his brother he must prove he can still wrestle and win over whoever comes across his path."[34] "Many of us wrestle with strangers in the night as we try to find the blessing we never had."[35]

Need we go on? Are these Promise Keepers authors really interpreting Scripture or are they simply reading their own psychologically-steeped presuppositions into Scripture? Scripture tells us to be diligent to show ourselves approved as workmen who need not be ashamed handling accurately the word of truth (2 Tim. 2:15). It is clear some Promise Keepers authors need to be more diligent.

Addicted to Love

Promise Keepers probably would have agreed with rock artist Robert Palmer who once sang "you might was well face it, you're addicted to love." Repeatedly, Promise Keepers writers and speakers describe sexual sin as though it were an addiction.

In *The Power of a Promise Kept*, we are introduced to a man named Kurt who, "(b)y his own admission . . . is a sex addict."[36] Although Kurt is said on at least one occasion to have a problem with "sexual sin," he is predominantly described as "having a problem with sexual addiction."[37]

Numerous articles in *New Man* also adopt the addiction model to describe sexual sin.[38] While some of these articles properly refer to sexual addiction as "sexual sin" or "adultery," typically the behavior is described as an "addiction," a "failure," a "habit," or a "trap." Few Bible verses appear in these articles, and when they do, they generally serve to illustrate some psychological principle or another.

We disagree with the use of the medical model of addiction to describe sexual sin, and our disagreement stems from three concerns. Our first concern is that the language of addiction is foreign to Scripture. Though addiction theorists attempt to impose the language of addiction on various passages, such as Paul's post-conversion confession in Romans 7:14-25, Scripture knows nothing of that language. Scripture speaks in moral and theological categories, not psychological. And just to set the record straight, the confession of Paul in Romans 7:14-25 is the confession of the *normal* Christian life as Galatians 5:17 also makes clear.

Our second concern is that the language of addiction is the language of victimization and at times, suggests that the one who is "addicted" is being acted upon by outside forces for which he is not responsible. In his fine book, *The Pursuit of Holiness*, Jerry Bridges looks with disfavor on describing sin in the language of "defeat," and his comments about "defeat" apply with equal force to descriptions of sin as an "addiction." When we say that we were *defeated* or that we are *addicted*, we are putting the blame on the sin. When, by contrast, we confess that we were and are *disobedient*, we put the blame where it belongs: on us as sinners.[39]

Our third concern is that the language of addiction and the medical model that it assumes tend to imply that the problem is typically beyond the reach of the pastor as he proclaims and ministers the Word of God to his congregation or biblically counsels individual members of the church. The language of addiction suggests that the one who is addicted needs the help of a mental health care professional—a professional counselor or therapist. Notwithstanding Promise 5 which attempts to affirm the role of the pastor in the local church, the language of addiction adopted by some Promise Keepers spokesmen actually undermines the role of the pastor in the local church by suggesting that he may not be competent to minister the Word of God to his people because they have a problem with addiction (the supposed domain of professional counselors and therapists) as opposed to sin (the supposed domain of pastors).

Dull Around the Edges

In *The Emperor's New Clothes*, Kilpatrick correctly notes that the "main practical effect of this psychological infiltration [in the church] has been a lowering of the consciousness of sin among Christians."[40] We hasten to add that with the "lowering of the consciousness of sin" comes a consequent lowering of a truly Christian response to sin wherever it may be found. The result is a dulling around the edges which, in turn, results in a lack of true integrity.

By contributing to the psychologized gospel of the late-twentieth century, Promise Keepers itself has had its consciousness of sin lowered. It also has had its own edges dulled, with the result of a compromised integrity. This compromise reached its peak not only with the publication of the highly psychologized book, *The Masculine Journey*, in 1993 but also with the subsequent reaction of Promise Keepers to the book's well-deserved criticisms. We take up these topics in the next chapter.

---

[1] Robert Liparulo, "Books," *New Man*, May/June, 1995, vol. 2, no. 3, p. 89.

[2] *Ibid.*, p. 90, quoting Peter Wilkes, *Winning the War Within* (InterVarsity Press).

[3] *New Man*, May/June, 1995, vol. 2, no. 3, p. 58, reprinted from *The Great Compromise* (Dallas, TX: Word, Inc., 1994).

[4] Quoted in *ibid.*

[5] Quoted in *ibid.*

[6] *Ibid.*

[7] William Kilpatrick, *The Emperor's New Clothes* (Westchester, IL: Crossway Books, 1986), p. 20 (hereafter *"TENC"*).

[8] *Ibid.*

[9] Anon., "I'll Do It Tomorrow," *New Man*, March/April, 1996, vol. 3, no. 2, p. 13.

[10] Smalley and Trent, *WMAM*, p. 44, 228.

[11] *WMAM*, p. 11.

[12] *WMAM*, p. 31.

[13] *Ibid.*, emphasis added.

[14] *TAPSB*, p. 149.

[15] *Ibid.*

[16] *TMJ*, p. 37.

[17] William Kilpatrick, *The Psychological Seduction: The Failure of Modern Psychology* (Nashville, TN: Thomas Nelson Publishers, 1983), p. 39.

[18] H.B. London, Jr., *SPPK*, p. 141.

[19] Michael C. Mack with Kevin Mitchell, adapted for the Small Group Network from *The Lookout*, December 4, 1994.

[20] *TMJSG*, pp. 15-16, emphasis added.

[21] *Ibid.*, p. 33.

[22] *Ibid.*

[23] Sarah H. Leslie, "Promise Keepers: 'Encountering' Guys at Risk," reprinted from *The Christian Conscience*, January, 1995, p. 1.

[24] *Ibid.*

[25] *Ibid.*

[26] *Ibid.*, p. 4.

[27] *Brothers!*, p. 38.

[28] *TMJ*, p. 105.

[29] Smalley and Trent, *WMAM*, pp. 39-40.

[30] *WMAM*, p. 63.

[31] *TMJ*, p. 114.

[32] *Ibid.*, p. 104.

[33] *Ibid.*, p. 117.

[34] *TMJSG*, p. 55.

[35] *TMJ*, p. 119; *TMJSG*, p. 56.

[36] *TPPK*, p. 115.

[37] *Ibid.*

[38] See, *e.g.*, Len LeSourd, "Escape the Sexual Trap," July/August, 1994, vol. 1, no. 1, pp. 46-48, 51-52; Archibald Hart, "Sex Under Control," November/December, 1994, vol. 1, no. 3, pp. 37-39; Don Crossland, "Escape from the Trap of Addiction," January/February, 1995, vol. 2, no. 1, pp. 52-54, 56; Anon., "The Story of a Former Adulterer," July/August, 1995, vol. 2, no. 4, pp. 55-57.

[39] Jerry Bridges, *The Pursuit of Holiness* (Colorado Springs, CO: Navpress, 1978), pp. 84-85.

[40] *TENC*, p. 21.

❊ SIX ❊

A Journey to Nowhere

Dorothy Parker once wrote a book review in which she quipped that the book was not one that should be put down lightly, but instead should be thrown with great force. So it is with *The Masculine Journey* by Robert Hicks, a book joint-ventured by Promise Keepers and Navpress, replete with psychobabble, secular men's movement theory, forced exegesis, and gross theological error parading as biblical truth.

Granted, Promise Keepers should have had the discernment not to have joint-ventured the book in the first place. But even when the storm of controversy erupted after the book's publication, Promise Keepers refused to do the right thing. Instead of tossing the book, Promise Keepers embraced it with open arms and continued to sell it for two years.

While we rejoice that Promise Keepers finally has begun to stiff-arm the book, we disagree with the damage control approach it has adopted which has kept it from retracting the book and admitting that it was wrong ever to have promoted it. When *public repentance* was the only fitting masculine response, Promise Keepers instead gave us only the pretty face of *public relations*. This is hardly what one would expect from the organization that would teach the rest of us how to become "men of integrity."

Setting the Stages

The fundamental premise of the book is that masculinity is not a static thing but a journey that is reflected in the six Hebrew terms for "man" found in the Old Testament reflecting the six stages of manhood: *'adam* (which Hicks defines as the creational male/the noble savage), *zakar* (the phallic male/the mysterious taskmaster), *gibbor* (the warrior/ the glorious hero), *enosh* (the wounded male/the painful incongruency), *ish* (the mature man/the reborn ruler), and *zaken* (the sage/the fulfilled man). According to Hicks, these words "say something very descriptive and normative about the masculine experience, which in turn helps us to delineate the meaning of manhood."[1] Though men can typify more than one stage at a time, the stages roughly follow a chronological progression. One cannot become a mature man, for example, without first becoming a wounded male. In this way, the book intends to provide a "roadmap" of sorts for the masculine journey.[2]

This thesis falls prey to several errors, the foremost of which is Hicks's unsubstantiated assumption that the use of different words necessarily implies normative stages of development. Consider a counter-example. By some counts, there are eight different Hebrew words for God. Are we therefore to assume, on Hicks's logic, that these different words for God necessarily imply different stages of godhood as some liberal process theologians have done? Of course not. Then why make that same assumption when it comes to the six Hebrew words for man?

Where, in fact, does this assumption come from? We don't have to guess. Hicks tells us. By his own admission, he started with a book written by secular men's movement theorist, Daniel Levinson, entitled, *The Seasons of a Man's Life*, going as far as commending it for its "excellent research." That "excellent research," however, consisted of taking an unrepresentative statistical sample of forty men between the ages of 35 and 45 who were interviewed by those Levinson himself admits were committed to the theories advanced by Freud, Jung, Erikson, Rank, Adler, and Reich.[3] These interviewers then collated the responses into "biographies" from which they developed generalizations that eventually became the "seasons" Levinson postulates.

But Hicks not only was attracted to *The Seasons of a Man's Life* because of its "excellent research," but also because, in his own words, "it fit my experience and the experience of so many other men . . ."[4] After having his eyes opened by Levinson and his own personal experience, coupled with that of others, Hicks *then* turned to the Scriptures to see if they had "anything to contribute in this regard," only to discover (surprise!) that the six Hebrew words roughly corresponded with the seasons described in Levinson's book.[5] Somehow concluding that "both the biblical material and the contemporary literature [secular men's movement literature] are amazingly close,"[6] Hicks conceived his thesis. After several centuries of this foolishness, you would think that Christians would have learned to stop using the Bible as decorative material for whatever the world thinks up.

The Gulf Between *Is* and *Ought*

Even assuming Hicks has correctly divined the meaning of the six Hebrew words he relies upon, nowhere does he explain how he moves from the *descriptive* (what he says *is* the case) to the *prescriptive* (what he says *ought* to be the case). He fallaciously assumes that the former implies the latter.

He also confuses the etymology of the Hebrew words under discussion with their meaning over time, overlooking the fact that words often mean one thing originally but then mean something completely different downstream. The English word *nice*, for example, originally meant "ignorant."

Today, it means "pleasant" or "delightful." If we were to do a study of the word *nice*, we would need to exercise extreme caution not to read our contemporary meaning into the term as it was originally used. Yet this is exactly what Hicks has done with the Hebrew words under discussion. He has read contemporary meanings back into the words under study; to be more specific, he has read contemporary men's movement theory back into the Bible. William Spencer, author of *The Goddess Revival* and an adjunct professor at Gordon-Conwell Theological Seminary, has pointed out that "Hicks has read thoroughly from the men's movement, and there are a lot of undigested ideas from that movement in the book."[7]

As but one illustration of how Hicks reads secular men's movement theory back into the words he claims to be defining, consider his claim that we, like the first Adam, are all "noble savages".[8] Though we are not fans of Margaret Mead's terminology ("noble savage"), even if we were to use it for a moment, we would see just how mistaken Hicks is when he claims that we are all noble savages today.

While the first Adam was created noble (upright), with savagery (rebellion) nowhere in sight, he *became* a savage by rebelling against God. And because he covenantally represented us all, what he did was imputed or credited to all of us as his heirs (Rom. 5:12-19). Hence, none of us is noble (upright) after the Fall. As opposed to Adam who was created noble (upright) in every respect, we are born savages (rebels) against God because we inherited the guilt, corruption, and pollution of Adam's sin. Whereas at creation, Adam was noble but not savage, today we are savage, but ignoble apart from Christ.

By Thy Words . . .

And this raises another criticism of the approach taken by Hicks. Far from presenting a *biblical* view of manhood and masculinity, all Hicks has done is present a lengthy word study of *man*. Word studies, while important, cannot stand on their own and often result in serious error if not balanced against a systematic understanding of what the Bible has to say about the concepts underlying the words being studied.

To illustrate, one of us once sat in on a study purportedly dealing with the biblical view of leadership. All the teacher did, however, was to look up the word *leader* every time it appeared in the Bible. His method was flawed from the outset. By focusing exclusively on the word *leader*, he missed every other passage that discussed the topic of leadership without using the term. Or take the doctrine of the Trinity as another illustration. Try doing a word study on *trinity*, and you will soon discover that the word *trinity* does not even appear in the Bible. Does that mean that the Bible does not teach the doctrine of the Trinity? Hardly. It just means that we cannot get at the truth of all biblical doctrines by limiting ourselves to word studies, the kind of study *The Masculine Journey* is based upon.

Word studies are only helpful in their own right when the words themselves are properly interpreted. While most *bona fide* Hebrew scholars would take issue with Hicks' study and the interpretations he foists on the words he studies, even assuming for the moment that Hicks has correctly defined the six Hebrew terms for "man," he has focused exclusively on the words themselves without balancing them against the systematic understanding of manhood, husbandry, and fatherhood taught in Scripture. As a result, he has not even come close to presenting the biblical view of manhood taught in Scripture.

In fact, Hicks's study is incomplete even from the standpoint of a word study since he never even bothers to discuss the New Testament Greek. The reason? It fails to support and completely eviscerates his thesis. The inspired authors of the New Testament had only two words (*anthropos* and

aner) at their disposal when quoting from the Greek translation of the Hebrew Old Testament known as the Septuagint.
Although Hebrew has a rich array of words for man (even
more than Hicks presents), the translators of the Septuagint
on whom the inspired writers of the New Testament de-
pended used only the two Greek words *anthropos* and *aner*.
Although a detailed analysis of the Greek would take us beyond the scope of this chapter, *aner* is used in the Septuagint,
to translate the Hebrew *ish*, *enosh*, *zaken*, *gibbor*, *baal*, *nasi*,
and *adon* and is rendered usually as *man*, but sometimes as
husband, warrior, prince, or *lord*. *Anthropos* is principally used
in the Septuagint to translate the Hebrew *'adam*, *ish*, and
enosh and is usually rendered *man*. What even this cursory
overview proves is that far from being packed with the eso-
teric meaning Hicks imputes to them, the various Hebrew
words he studies are commonly synonymns for *man*. They
carry no signification of normative development, as Hicks
imagines. Simply put, Hicks's thesis does not square with
the data of Scripture. He has foisted his thesis on Scripture.

"But," protests the supporter of Hicks's thesis, "the limi-
tations of Greek shouldn't be imposed on Hebrew." This
objection misses the point. The point is not that the Greek
limits the Hebrew, but that the Septuagint and the inspired
authors of the New Testament who quoted from the
Septuagint, did not attach the significance Hicks attaches to
the Hebrew words Hicks discusses, thereby indicating that
to them, the words were simply synonymous for *man*. Had
the Hebrew terms meant what Hicks proposes they mean,
the translators of the Septuagint and the New Testament
writers could have used modifiers when translating them, as
they did in several other places when describing a particular
type of man. Instead of translating *enosh* as simply *man*, for
instance, they could have translated it as *wounded warrior*
and so on. This they never did with any of the six Hebrew
words, thus showing that they did not construe them as
signifying some kind of divinely inspired normative devel-

opment. And we believe they knew more about the correct interpretation of Hebrew than does Hicks.

Off the Deep End

Aside from these flaws which strike at the very heart of *The Masculine Journey*, other flaws reveal that the book has little, if anything, to do with the true view of manhood taught in Scripture. Consider the following representative illustrations taken from the book and its accompanying study guide:

- "For me, the only way to understand the concept of self-esteem as something to be valued is to ground it in the 'image of God.'"[9] "As men, we have value because we merely *are*, not because of what we do or accomplish . . . . I have value for no other reason than just being."[10] "Only God's radical grace can free us from thinking that it's what we do, not who we are, that matters most to God."[11]

Although we have dealt with the unbiblical concept of self-esteem in the previous chapter, we note here that Hicks is right when he says that it is not what we do that commends us to God. But, contrary to Hicks, who we *are* outside of Christ makes no difference either. Apart from Christ we do evil because we are evil. We are not "noble savages," as Hicks would have us believe. After the Fall, there is nothing noble about us at all. The image of God safeguards the sanctity of life; it does not provide a foothold for self-esteem theory. It is not what we do or who we are that matters to God. It is what Christ did and who He is that matters to God. He is our only hope and the only One who can restore the image of God in us by redeeming us as His people.

- "In the woman *'adam* sees himself, one human to another but utterly different from *the other animals*."[12]

Notice how Hicks classifies human beings created in

the image of God with "other animals." No wonder, since
only five pages earlier he approvingly quotes Charles Dar-
win who, in *The Descent of Man*, wrote that "Man with all
his noble qualities still bears in his bodily frame the indel-
ible stamp of his lowly origin."[13] Nothing could be further
from a truly biblical anthropology. Adam did not have a
lowly origin. He was created upright but subsequently fell
into sin.

• When speaking about men who have avoided an effeminate Christianity and who have pursued other interests
in life rather than joining the church, Hicks writes: "I personally don't blame them. I think it speaks highly of them."[14]

Hicks has blurred some serious lines here. Rebellion
against the King of kings never speaks highly of anyone.
Sadly, the church has been neutered, but only because men
pursued other interests and chose not to exercise the covenant headship granted to them by God. Ironically, what
Hicks admires in such men is the very problem he is condemning.

• "(T)his word [*zakar*] reflects the *phallic male* in his
distinct sexual aspect. . . . We are sexual beings at our most
primary (primal) level. . . . To be a male is to be a phallic
kind of guy. . . . The Bible simply defines manhood by the
phallus. . . ."[15]

This is fallacious reductionism at its worst. Doesn't man
have a spiritual as well as a physical aspect to his being?
Without denigrating the physical aspect of our being, doesn't
Scripture repeatedly teach us that we are spiritual beings at
our most primal level (*e.g.*, Matt. 10:28; 1 Tim. 4:8)? Upon
what basis, then, can Hicks conclude that the sexual aspect
of our being is the most primal?

• "Possessing a penis places unique requirements upon
men before God in how they are to worship Him. We are

called to worship God as phallic kinds of guys, not as some sort of androgynous, neutered nonmales, or the feminized males so popular in many feminist-enlightened churches. We are told by God to worship Him in accordance with what we are, phallic men."[16]

We are called to worship God in spirit and in truth (Jn. 4:24), not as "phallic kinds of guys" (whatever that means). Since His Word is truth (Jn. 17:17), His Word prescribes the kind of worship that is pleasing to Him. While men and women have different functions to perform in worship (*e.g.*, 1 Cor. 14:34; 1 Tim. 2:11-15), even those functional distinctions are not ultimately based upon anatomy but upon creation and the Fall (1 Tim. 2:13-15). Headship at home and at church belongs to men. Hicks is simply confusing masculinity with the phallus.

• "As men we must accept our sexuality as normal, not abnormal. We must learn to worship God with our sexuality. This means living to honor God with our phallus in the context of the restraints He has prescribed."[17]

Hicks has not exercised the caution that his subject matter demands. He no doubt is well aware of the fact that the Bible uses the word worship in a broad and narrow sense. In the broad sense, we are to worship God—to serve Him—as a way of life. Romans 12:1-2 has this broad sense of worship in view when it tells us to present our bodies as living sacrifices, as a spiritual service of worship. But the Bible also speaks of worship in the narrow sense to mean special acts of reverence we offer to Him in holy assembly with His people in accordance with His Word. By suggesting that we need to "worship God with our sexuality," Hicks presumably means worship in the broad sense; we are to honor and serve Him in all we do, including the sexual aspect of our being. Were Hicks to mean worship in the narrow sense (as in the quotations immediately above), he would be advocating the rank paganism and fertility cult worship so resoundingly condemned throughout the Bible. Not only does Hicks fail to define what he means by worship, he also fails to define what he means by accepting our sexuality as *normal*. If, by *normal*, he means the way we have been created by God, then he is closer to the truth. If, by contrast, he means sexual practices, then normalcy is irrelevant. Our standard is not what is normal. Our standard is Christ.

• "I'm sure many would balk at my thought of celebrating the experience of sin. I'm not sure how we could do it. But I do know we need to do it. For example, we usually give the teenagers in our churches such a massive dose of condemnation regarding their first experiences with sin that I sometimes wonder how any of them recover. Maybe we could take a different approach. Instead of jumping all over them when they have their first experience with the police, or their first drunk, or their first experience with sex or drugs, we could look upon this as a teachable moment and a rite of passage. Is this putting a benediction on sin? Of course not, but perhaps at this point the true elders could come forward and confess their own adolescent sins and congratulate the next generation for being human. Then they could move on to the all-important issues of forgiveness and restoration, but this time on common ground, with the young person as a fellow sinner!"[18]

While we comment on this text in subsequent chapters, we pause here only to make a few points. We are not called to congratulate, condone or coddle young people who are given to gross immorality; we are called to correct them in love. Moreover, we should never manipulate young people. We should take them to the Word of God lovingly but pointedly in order to drive them to Christ as their only hope of salvation and the pattern of the good works that should flow from sanctification, if indeed, He has begun His good work in them. Furthermore, when young people are given to sin, they are not the only parties covenantally responsible before God. So are their parents (1 Sam. 3:13; Prov. 22:6; Tit. 1:6). Finally, since when do we need to begin celebrating the experience of sin and how can we do so without encouraging it? Is the opposite of condemning sin celebrating it? Where is the biblical balance of correcting in love?

• "Current Christianity cannot openly deal with or talk about the male phallus in its full sexual activity or fantasy."[19] "As men, the phallus defines our identity."[20] "I believe Jesus was phallic with all the inherent phallic passions we experience as men. But it was never recorded that Jesus had sexual relations with a woman. He may have thought about it as the movie *The Last Temptation of Christ* portrays, but even in the movie He did not give in to the temptation and remained true to His messianic course. If temptation means anything, it means Christ was tempted in *every* way as we are. That would mean not only heterosexual temptation but also homosexual temptation! I have found this insight to be very helpful for gay men struggling with their sexuality."[21]

Several problems are revealed in these comments. To begin with, Hicks does not present the biblical view of Christ. To say that He was tempted in every way and was yet without sin is not to say that He experienced every single instance of temptation we experience today. Would Hicks also suggest that our Lord (as Paul would say, we are insane to talk like this!) was tempted with other gross forms of sexual perversion known to man as well? While our Lord experienced every category of temptation, He did not necessarily experience every instance of temptation (homosexual, bestial, *etc.*). Some temptations can only exist with a prior pattern of disobedience and rebellion. Furthermore, *The Last Temptation* was rather lurid and is not a good source for distinguishing the difference between temptation and sin. In the end, Hicks has denigrated the Lord of Glory in order to exalt man.

• "A man cannot become the ruler of his own soul and genuine in his relationships until he has been through some wounding."[22] "Alcoholic fathers, dysfunctional families, divorce after one or two years of marriage, and multiple job firings are all wounding men at earlier ages. At men's conferences and retreats, more and more young men are coming up after my sessions and telling me their stories of abuse, aloneness, chemical dependencies, and inadequate relationships with women. Some take desperate leaps for young men and reveal their guilt and anxiety about being gay or about being straight and addicted to sex or pornography. . . . My reply to them is, 'Your wound is honorable; your wound is a normal part of male development. Life is not over. This wound may be the entry point for new wisdom and power; it may be the voice of God. Now we need to figure out what it means and how to move toward healing in order to keep you on the masculine journey. We need to help you find a way out of your inappropriate response to some abnormal event or circumstance in your past.' It's but a momentary stop on the map of manhood."[23]

Hicks has gone too far. It is crucial for Hicks to prove that all men are wounded since men cannot become mature until they have come out on the other side of the wounding experience. Hicks' model drives his analysis and leads to numerous errors. First, Hicks' model is suspect in its own right, as pointed out earlier in this chapter. What Hicks in some places calls *wounding* the Bible simply calls suffering, and it is not limited to men. God can and does use human suffering to cause us to grow in Him, but it is not the *sina qua non* for growth or maturity in the Christian life. Second, much of what Hicks calls wounding the Bible calls sin. We may not be responsible for every hardship we experience (*e.g.*, the child who grows up with an alcoholic father), but we are responsible for the sin-induced hardships we experience (divorce, job firings, chemical dependencies, homosexuality, adultery, and pornography). Third, sin is never honorable. We are never to sin that grace may abound (Rom. 6:1). We never do evil that good may come (Rom. 3:8). If God, by His grace, is pleased to convert a sinner by using a "wound" brought on by sinfulness, then praise be to His holy name. But even then, the sin itself is never honorable. Fourth, "wounding" (read: gross immorality) is never "a normal part of male development" as Hicks imagines. Besides, Hicks is begging the question as to what the standard is. Is our standard the holy law of God which reveals our sin, or is it some man-centered notion of normalcy? Fifth, Hicks euphemizes sin by calling it an "inappropriate response" *en route* to laying the blame for the sin on "some abnormal event or circumstance in your past." He ends up advocating therapeutic moralism as a substitute for the gospel of justification by grace alone through faith alone on account of Christ alone. At the very point when the sinner needs to be confronted with the demands of the law, his sinfulness, and his need for the perfect righteousness of Christ alone, Hicks coddles him and basically tells him "It's okay, we'll figure something out."

Which Way Did He Go?

Based on the erroneous teachings found in *The Masculine Journey*, only some of which have been highlighted in this chapter, Promise Keepers has recently attempted to distance itself from the book in a very discreet fashion: it no longer sells the book. Yet Promise Keepers has not come out and publicly retracted its earlier support of the book. While Promise Keepers is moving in the right direction, its recent reaction is too little, too late.

Some have suggested that the whole controversy is like a child that should never have been laid at the doorstep of Promise Keepers. On the contrary, the facts reveal a different story. Promise Keepers has fathered the child and now no longer wants to take responsibility for what it has done. To see why this is the case, let's look at the facts. For starters, the book is stamped with the official Promise Keepers logo. As the registered owner of that logo, Promise Keepers has a legal responsibility to license usage of it. Only those who are licensed by Promise Keepers can use it. Promise Keepers licensed and authorized the use of its logo on the book, thereby sanctioning the book's contents.

Not only does the book bear the symbol of the movement, but the book was also distributed by Promise Keepers to the 50,000 men that crowded into Boulder's Folsom Stadium for the 1993 Promise Keepers conference. In addition, Hicks was one of the featured conference speakers. Thus, Promise Keepers has sanctioned Hicks's message in both written and verbal form.

The last page of the book describes the Promise Keepers movement and unabashedly endorses the book by saying "Promise Keepers wants to provide men's materials (*like this book*) as well as seminars and the annual conference to emphasize the godly conviction, integrity, and action each of us needs."[24] In other words, Promise Keepers endorses this book and wants to provide even more books like it in the future.

The book also received glowing endorsements from some of Promise Keepers' most well known speakers. Howard G. Hendricks, for instance, wrote that "(n)o matter how long you have studied the Bible, you will find *The Masculine Journey* an eye-opening key to understanding the Bible's teaching on what it means to be a man."[25] Gary Oliver exclaims, "With forthrightness and clarity, Bob Hicks courageously tackles some of the most important issues facing men today. This book is insightful, fresh, and challenging—a must read."[26] And John Trent confesses,

> I wish I had a copy of this book when I was a young man, grappling with what biblical masculinity really was. I'm

thankful that I have it now. Whether you're a young man, defining yourself by your strength; in middle age fighting to build correct priorities; or in your latter years, seeking to stay the course, *The Masculine Journey* offers wisdom and encouragement.[27]

Even after the storm of controversy over the book erupted, Promise Keepers issued a detailed letter written by Pete Richardson, Vice President, Communications Services, defending the book and Promise Keepers' endorsement of it. And it is this letter that gives rise to an even deeper concern. While Promise Keepers showed a tremendous blind spot by joint-venturing and promoting the book in the first place, its failure to do the right thing when the obvious blunders of the book were brought to light is even more deplorable.

The official letter defending the book identifies the real culprit: the critic. The problem is not with the content of the book, but "in the way that the book is read."[28] In other words, the blunders in the book are not Hicks's fault. They are ours. We are imagining them. As opposed to these imagined blunders, Promise Keepers assures us that the book presents

> a biblically-centered, frank and honest account of a man's journey with God. We were convinced that it would help men pursue Jesus Christ amidst the challenges of the twentieth century. . . . We endorsed it because we believed that it would be a tool that challenged men to grow in Christlikeness, to become *zaken* or wise men of God, as Hicks writes.[29]

A Question of Integrity

Apparently, Promise Keepers no longer believes its own statement since the organization reportedly no longer sells the book. The problem here is one of discernment. The fact that the Promise Keepers could ever have endorsed the book reveals that the organization may lack the discernment necessary to play the vital role it currently enjoys in the lives of thousands upon thousands of men and their families. But the problem is also one of integrity.

Promise Keepers spokesman, Steve Chavis, was recently reported to have said that the controversies surrounding *The Masculine Journey* and other concerns about the Promise Keepers movement are frustrating diversions from the real work of Promise Keepers.[30] If accurate, this statement reveals something just as disturbing as the doctrinal errors that gave rise to the criticisms in the first place: the tendency to look at doctrine as a diversion, as something that should be minimized so that the "real work" of the Lord can be done.

It is not surprising that Chavis responded in this way since Promise Keepers president, Randy Phillips, shares the same view. When asked whether Promise Keepers ever planned on addressing doctrinal issues that have traditionally divided Roman Catholics and Protestants (such as the definition of the gospel), Phillips responded by saying "I think you're dealing with a whole area that is not our expertise or calling."[31]

In other words, Phillips is saying that teaching doctrine is not the calling of Promise Keepers. To see how untenable Phillips' position is, just substitute the phrase "the teachings of the Scriptures" for the word "doctrine" as E. Glenn Wagner, Vice President of Ministry Advancement for Promise Keepers, has done in *The Awesome Power of Shared Beliefs*.[32] What Phillips is really saying is that the teachings of the Scriptures are not the expertise or the calling of Promise Keepers.

If teaching doctrine is not the expertise or the calling of Promise Keepers, then Promise Keepers is in the wrong business. Apparently, Phillips and Chavis don't realize that when you purport to teach the Bible, doctrine is paramount and unavoidable. The issue is not whether or not Promise Keepers teaches doctrine. The issue is really whether or not it teaches true doctrine. And that is simply another way of asking whether what is taught is consistent with Scripture. To attempt to push off doctrinal issues as unimportant or diversionary because we want to spend our time "doing the work of the Lord" is to miss the whole point: we cannot set about doing the work of the Lord until we first understand what that work is all about. In order to have that understanding, we need to know what the Bible teaches and be able to teach it faithfully to others.

And this raises the real concern with Promise Keepers' lackluster response to the whole fiasco surrounding *The Masculine Journey*: Promise Keepers refuses to take responsibility for the false doctrine it has taught or promulgated. To promulgate *The Masculine Journey* (or any of the other errors detailed in this book) and then label as divisive those who care enough to bring those errors to your attention is simply a cheap shot. The implication is all too clear: *our critics* are worried about doctrine, while *we* are the ones doing the real work of the Lord. Not only is this reasoning intellectually dishonest, it is also laden with arrogance.

Ironically, Promises Keepers condemns authoritarianism in the church, but then turns around and sets itself up as an unassailable authority. To question Promise Keepers is to raise suspicion of your *bona fides* as a Christian man in some circles. You are seen as getting in the way of the real work of the Lord. As evangelical observer, Michael Horton, has commented

> Already to criticize Promise Keepers at any point is to be charged with getting in God's way. And although these movements pride themselves on creating a united church and refuse to allow doctrine to divide, they're very willing to divide Christians over whether one accepts the movement as being of God.[33]

By deflecting justifiable concerns about errors Promise Keepers has promoted as biblical truth, the very organization that purports to teach us about becoming "men of integrity" has itself demonstrated a total lack of true integrity. It has refused to take responsibility for what it has done wrong. True men of integrity teach even their children that privileges come with corresponding responsibilities.

The privilege of teaching the Word of God is no different; it comes with a corresponding responsibility to "Study to show thyself approved unto God, a workman that needeth not to be ashamed, rightly dividing the word of truth" (2 Tim. 2:15). Or, as James puts it, "Let not many of you become teachers, my brethren, knowing that as such we shall incur a stricter judgment" (3:1). If Promise Keepers doesn't want to take responsibility for teaching error, then it shouldn't avail itself of the privilege of teaching the Word of God in the first place. But if it does avail itself of that privilege, then it should have the integrity to admit publicly when it has erred. Public relations might calm some fears here on earth. But, according to James, it will not suffice on the day of judgment.

---

[1] *TMJ*, p. 20.

[2] *Ibid.*, p. 14.

[3] *The Seasons of a Man's Life* (New York, NY: Ballantine Books, 1978), p. 14.

[4] *TMJ*, p. 19.

[5] *Ibid.*

[6] *Ibid.*, p. 105.

[7] Quoted in Doug LeBlanc, "The Masculine Journey of Promise Keepers," *The Christian Research Journal*, Fall, 1995, vol. 18, no. 2, p. 7.

[8] *Ibid.*, p. 32.

[9] *Ibid.*, p. 36.

[10] *Ibid.*, pp. 37-38.

[11] *TMJSG*, p. 26.

[12] *Ibid.*, p. 35, emphasis added.

[13] *Ibid.*, p. 31.

[14] *Ibid.*, p. 34.

[15] *Ibid.*, pp. 24, 49.

[16] *Ibid.*, p. 51.

[17] *Ibid.*, p. 69.

[18] *Ibid.*, p. 177.

[19] *Ibid.*, p. 54.

[20] *Ibid.*, p. 68.

[21] *Ibid.*, p. 181.

[22] *Ibid.*, p. 26.

[23] *Ibid.*, p. 108.

[24] *Ibid.*, p. 203, emphasis added.

[25] *Ibid.*, back cover.

[26] *Ibid.*

[27] *Ibid.*

[28] Quoted in Anon., "Promise Keepers: Ecumenical 'Macho-Men' for Christ?" (n.d.), p. 11.

[29] Quoted in Martin and Deidre Bobgan, *Promise Keepers & PsychoHeresy* (Santa Barbara, CA: PsychoHeresy Awareness Ministries, 1994), p. 33.

[30] LeBlanc, "The Masculine Journey of Promise Keepers," p. 46.

[31] Albert James Dager, "Promise Keepers: Is What You See What You Get?", *Media Spotlight* (Special Report, 1994), p. 11.

[32] *TAPSB*, p. xiv.

[33] Horton, "What About the Promise Keepers Movement?", *The White Horse Inn* radio broadcast, tape no. WHI-237 (Anaheim, CA: C.U.R.E., 1995).

❖ SEVEN ❖

Tying Up Some Loose Ends

Before delving into the specific concerns arising from the seven promises themselves, we need to round out our look at some of the general concerns arising from the Promise Keepers movement as a whole.

Going Along with the Crowd

In 1821, an attorney in New York was dramatically converted and almost immediately left his law practice to begin pleading the cause of Christ in the course of what has come to be known as the Second Great Awakening. His name was Charles Finney, and he profoundly altered the landscape of American evangelism by changing the focus of the message proclaimed from God to man. The shift was from a declaration of the person and work of Christ to motivational speeches urging listeners to pull themselves up by their own spiritual bootstraps.

Rejecting the doctrines of original sin and the substitutionary atonement of Christ, Finney employed what came to be called "New Measures" and bragged that if his methods were followed, they would (with near scientific certainty) result in conversion for at least some of his listeners. For Finney, technique not truth, skill not sovereign grace, were the heartbeat of evangelism. He left a legacy for many evangelists to come. Who could forget Billy Sunday's "gospel of manhood," or D. L. Moody's program of "muscular Christianity," both of which owed much to Finney and served as precursors to the Promise Keepers movement.

Despite Finney's focus on man rather than God as the causative agent in salvation, some Promise Keepers speakers and writers hold Finney up as a model for the rest of us to follow today. Says one Promise Keepers author, "God still needs men who, like . . . Charles Finney, will give themselves to prayer and then go and do whatever the Holy Spirit tells them."[1] This plea, of course, begs the question as to whether the Holy Spirit told Finney to do the things that Finney did. But even more importantly, it reveals something very profound about Promise Keepers—that Promise Keepers has no problems with Finney. Indeed, it has given itself to some "New Measures" all its own.

From the very outset, Bill McCartney has thought in terms of numbers. Here's how the nearly-apocryphal story of the beginnings of Promise Keepers is usually told in Promise Keepers promotional material:

> On March 20, 1990, Bill McCartney (at the time, University of Colorado Head Football Coach) and his friend Dave Wardell, Ph.D. were on a three-hour car ride to a Fellowship of Christian Athletes meeting in Pueblo, CO, when the idea of filling a stadium with Christian men first came up. Later in 1990, seventy-two men began to pray and fast about the concept of thousands of men coming together for the purpose of Christian discipleship.[2]

From the beginning, the goal was to attract a large number of men to a stadium conference. And Promise Keepers admits that technique is all-important at the numerous conferences men now attend:

As the praise and worship music from the Maranatha!
Promise Band *sets the tone* for each conference, one feels
the presence of the Spirit of God.[3]

Setting the tone is the key not only of the larger stadium-
styled conferences, but also of the small groups that meet
after the conferences. An official Promise Keepers study guide
on small groups tells us that *"the atmosphere you create is more
important than the content that you cover."*[4]

Perhaps this Finney-like focus on technique ("atmosphere") over truth ("content") explains why at least one
Promise Keepers conference early on featured Charles
Swindoll riding into the stadium on a Harley to the tune of
"Born to be Wild," or why Gary Smalley, not to be out-
done, chose to make his entrance on a tricycle. And we would
be remiss if we neglected to mention the other typical crowd
pleasers: styrofoam gliders, paper airplanes, large beachballs,
high fives, back slaps, the wave, the token motivation speech
by the sports-star-turned-amateur-theologian, and all the rest.

With all the fun and frolic of a typical conference which
one sympathizer has described as "emotionally charged manhood,"[5] we need to stop and ask ourselves if the large numbers really mean anything more than that the "right" tech-
niques are being employed, *i.e.*: whether the crude "science"
begun by Finney now has been perfected in the Promise
Keepers laboratory.

Some might object by asking, "But doesn't the rapid
growth of the movement over such a short period of time
necessarily prove that it is 'born in the heart of God' or
'truly blessed by God?'"

Not necessarily.

Just think of some religious cults that make the same
claim given their rapid growth in recent years. Now we are
not comparing Promise Keepers to a cult; we are merely
questioning the idea that numbers determine theological
truth. Does the rapid growth of the cults prove they too are

"born in the heart of God" or that they are "truly blessed by God"? They would like to think so, but we know differently. How so? Because our standard for measuring all movements or groups is the Word of God. When a fast-growing cult is measured against that standard, it comes up short. Since we know that God cannot contradict His Word, we know that the growth we see in cults is not from God at all, despite what its adherents might say. And we also shouldn't forget that some of their adherents were drawn to them unaware of what they really teach. They are drawn in spite of what the cults really teach, and not because of it.

Are we suggesting that Promise Keepers is cultic? Absolutely not. We are simply saying that supporters of the Promise Keepers movement cannot necessarily appeal to numbers to prove anything, any more than cults can. Numbers do not tell us anything about the truth. To illustrate this point again, look at the world's population *vis-à-vis* Christianity: by some counts, more than two-thirds of that population is non-Christian. Does that necessarily prove anything about the truth of various forms of the non-Christian worldview or the falsity of the Christian worldview? Of course not.

The same reasoning applies to the popularity of Promise Keepers. Promise Keepers may attract large numbers of men, but that fact alone does not prove that everything it teaches is true. Nor does it somehow prove that the movement is necessarily blessed of God, or that even if blessed, that the movement is somehow immune from sound biblical scrutiny.

The Medicine Man

One of the reasons why men flock to Promise Keepers conferences in the first place is because they are told that they will find answers there to all of life's perplexing questions. Along these lines, some in the movement are fond of saying that if Jesus is the answer, the question must be wounded egos, broken marriages, neglected children, alcohol, drugs, and the like.

While Christ Himself is *the* answer and, through his indwelling Spirit, enables us to overcome various trials and temptations, we should exercise extreme caution before saying or implying that if we come to Christ all of our problems will miraculously vanish.

Jesus is indeed the answer to life's trials and tribulations in the sense that He strengthens us, blesses us, and causes us to grow through them. But He doesn't promise to take them away from us. In fact, He warned His followers that they might suffer terrible persecution for His sake, possibly even *strife* in the home (Matt. 5:10-12; 10:34-36). Sometimes the Lord brings harmony into a home. Other times the Lord brings controversy. Christ is not the medicine man dispensing His miraculous panacea to all takers. He is the sovereign Lord of the universe who knows what is best for His children.

Reinventing the Wheel

The medicine man approach is so appealing because we do have a lot of unanswered questions. But one of the reasons why we have so many questions and so few answers is because we have fallen prey to the notion that we have nothing to learn from those who have provided satisfactory answers in times past. We are guilty, as C. S. Lewis once remarked, of "chronological snobbery," the fallacious assumption that what is newer is necessarily better or truer.

Promise Keepers, perhaps unwittingly, reflects this chronological snobbery. Seldom does the movement point us backward to learn what saints of old had to say about the biblical view of manhood, husbandry, and fatherhood. Instead, Promise Keepers caters to the modern craving for the new-fangled by writing *new* books, producing *new* study guides, and composing *new* songs.

Now, it is true that we can be guilty of the opposite error: the fallacious assumption that what is older is better or truer. Nevertheless, we should always keep in mind that creativity is not necessarily a virtue in theology. The real point in this discussion is that the standard for determining what is true is not *age*, but *Scripture*. And if we strive for scriptural truth, we will welcome it no matter how old it may be. We must also be humble enough to admit that sometimes those who have preceded us may have done a better job than we can do today.

So it is with the rich theology of the family. While some contemporary literature on the family is truly biblical and edifying, some of the best material is hundreds of years old. But we will never learn what this material says if we dismiss it from the beginning as being antiquated. Nor will we learn what it says if we refuse to take time to read and study it because MTV is so much more entertaining. Sometimes we dismiss those who have preceded us, knowing what they had to say but thinking that it just can't speak to us modern sophisticates. At other times, however, we don't even know what they had to say because, in the words of Neil Postman, we have been too busy "amusing ourselves to death."

Admit it. We have been chronological snobs, and we have been having a jolly good time. Either way, the end result is the same: we end up trying to reinvent the wheel, only to discover that what we have come up with doesn't roll very well after all. Never knowing that wheels actually rolled in times past, we clop along merrily, thinking that this square "wheel" of ours is pretty great.

We have no excuse. All we have to do is open our eyes. Then we should get on our knees.

The Humpty Dumpty Syndrome

Who could forget the memorable interchange between Alice and Humpty Dumpty in Lewis Carroll's *Through the Looking Glass*. At one point, Alice protests Humpty's bizarre use of words. "When I use a word," responded Humpty in a rather scornful tone, "it means just what I choose it to mean—neither more nor less." Getting the better of him, Alice retorts, "The question is . . .whether you can make words mean so many different things."

After seeing how some Promise Keepers speakers and writers press Scripture into service to justify all sorts of teachings, one is left to ask Alice's penetrating question all over again—whether Promise Keepers can make the words of Scripture mean so many different things. We call this problem the Humpty Dumpty syndrome, and it is more prevalent than most would care to admit.

While this book elsewhere details many questionable uses of Scripture by the Promise Keepers, there are a few examples of carelessness that deserve special treatment at this point.

Crooked Arrows

Consider as but one example Promise Keepers president, Randy Phillips, who, during at least one 1995 conference, taught the story of Joash and Elisha (2 Kings 13:1-19) as a prelude to inviting 60,000 men to commit themselves to the seven promises.

As you will recall, Joash came to Elisha weeping over Syria's oppression of Israel (v. 14). Elisha told him to take a bow and arrows, to point the bow eastward, and to shoot an arrow (vv. 15-17). When Joash complied, Elisha used this object lesson to encourage Joash by exclaiming, "The Lord's arrow of victory, even the arrow of victory over Syria; for you shall defeat the Syrians" (v. 17). Then Elisha told Joash to take the arrows and strike the ground. Joash complied but only struck the ground three times. Elisha, sensing an apparent lack of faith, became angry and told Joash that he should have struck the ground "five or six times" (v. 19), thereby demonstrating his faith that God would completely destroy Syria. Because he only struck the ground three times, Israel would defeat Syria, but not completely destroy it (vv. 18-19).

Based on this text, Phillips encouraged the men in the stadium to raise their hands and to clench their fists as if they, like Joash, had arrows in them. He then read each of the seven promises to them and asked them to affirm their commitment to each one by bringing their arms down as if they were going to "strike the ground" with their clenched fists, saying "Yes Jesus" each time.

According to Phillips, the encounter between Joash and Elisha teaches us to become promise keepers by "striking the ground" seven times with what amounts to an Atlanta Braves tomahawk chop, Promise Keepers style.

Needless to say, Phillips has wrested the passage from its context and allegorized it in a way that would have made medieval monks blush. At the same time, he turns the passage into a twentieth-century ritual, clenched fists and all. But why stop there? Next time, why not have all the men in the stadium march down to the nearest river and bathe seven times as Naaman did a few chapters earlier (2 Kings 5:1-14)? At least the story of Naaman uses the number seven!

Hugs and Kisses

A few months before Phillips invited his listeners to "strike the ground" with the seven promises, Rod Cooper, the National Director of Education for Promise Keepers, wrote an article in *New Man* about what he calls "the blessing," which he defines as "[a] sense of being nurtured, a feeling of significance and security that only a man can give to another man."[6] He then observes that "[t]oo many men didn't receive the blessing from their fathers."[7]

While some would question the merits of his argument

in its own right, he provides them with additional fodder by "quoting" Scripture to support his argument. Somehow, he comes up with the story of Esau:

> The Old Testament says Esau grieved when he lost his birthright. But notice *what* he grieved: "Bless me, too, father." Esau was devastated because he did not receive the blessing. Men have a God-given need to be blessed and affirmed. They get this through relationship.[8]

Cooper notwithstanding, the story of Esau is not a story about fatherly affirmation. It is a story about covenantal succession. Esau grieved because he realized that selling his birthright was an outward sign that he was outside the covenant with God and the blessings that flowed from it. He was a reprobate, and he knew it.

The apostle Paul himself taught about the lives of Jacob and Esau in his epistle to the Romans. In chapter 9, Paul, under inspiration of the Holy Spirit, gives us a divine commentary of the life of Jacob and Esau and tells us indirectly why Esau grieved. According to Paul, God loved Jacob but hated Esau:

> for though the twins [Jacob and Esau] were not yet born and had not done anything good or bad, in order that God's purpose according to His choice might stand, not because of works, but because of Him who calls, it was said to her, "The older [Esau] will serve the younger [Jacob]." Just as it is written "Jacob I loved, but Esau I hated" (Rom. 9: 11-13).

Esau recognized that by selling his birthright for a mess of pottage, he thereby demonstrated that he was a God-hater and was hated by God. Getting a hug from daddy was not what was on Esau's mind. Esau forfeited the covenant blessing of God and found himself to be an outsider to that covenant. He was a covenant-breaker. The "blessing" he longed for was not male affection (whatever that means). It was divine affection, the very affection he already had forfeited. So he grieved, although as a profane man he grieved on his own terms.

Should brothers encourage one another in the body of Christ? Absolutely. But that is not the point of the passage cited. Cooper wrongfully presses the story of Esau into service and uses it as a proof text for "the blessing" just because the passage uses the word "blessing." He incorrectly assumes that the passage uses "blessing" as *he* has defined that phrase. Simply put, he equivocates on the meaning of "blessing," and in the end, simply reads his own meaning into the text.

Taking a Stand

In the same issue of *New Man*, yet another example of the misuse of Scripture is found in a story about the well-respected and highly talented Desmond Armstrong. After unexpectedly and unjustifiably getting cut from the American soccer team, Armstrong commendably refused to wallow around in self-pity. Instead, he admirably allowed himself to be used by God by making the best of the unfortunate situation. But listen to the text of the Bible he supposedly relied upon and the lesson he infers from it:

> Jesus is on a boat with His disciples. A big storm comes and the disciples are in a panic. Jesus is asleep. It says in the Bible they all went over to wake Him. The first thing He did was to *stand up*. For me, that means He's a man of action. He didn't just sit and allow the storm to run rampant. He got up and did something about it.[9]

So Armstrong applied this lesson to his life; instead of having an adult-sized pity party after getting cut from the team, he stood up like Jesus and became a man of action.

But did Christ stand in the boat to provide an object lesson for us to "stand up" to life's trials or is Armstrong improperly using a literal truth (that Christ stood) as a meta-

phor for life (standing up to life's trials)? Christ also slept at
the beginning of the storm. Is He thereby teaching us that if
we would really be men of action, we should sleep before
the storms of life arise?

Should we stand up and be counted as men of God? Sure.
Should we become men of action? Certainly. But we
shouldn't think that the account of Christ standing in the
boat teaches us this important truth.

Loosening the Laces

Shortly after the article on Armstrong made its way into
print, Jack Hayford exhorted men at the 1995 Promise Keepers conference at Denver's Mile High Stadium from Exodus
3, which records the burning bush encounter between God
and Moses. In this passage, God appeared to Moses in the
burning bush, and when Moses approached Him, He told
Moses to take his sandals off because the ground upon which
he stood was holy. Those who heard the message were encouraged to apply this truth to their lives and responded by
literally taking off their shoes.

Capturing the highlights of the 1995 conference season,
New Man preserved a snapshot of one promise keeper in
Denver with the caption: "A Promise Keeper takes off his
shoes in response to Jack Hayford's message on worship."[10]
Apparently, the same message was preached in Indianapolis
the next week, since just two pages later in *New Man*, we see
a whole group of men with shoes off in front of them, and a
caption that reads "Men remove their shoes in reverence."[11]

We certainly need to have more reverence today. Much
of the problem of contemporary evangelicalism is that somewhere along the way, we evangelicals stopped believing that
"(i)t is a fearful thing to fall into the hands of the living God"
(Heb. 10:31), and that we are to work out our salvation "with
fear and trembling" (Phil. 2:12-13). In short, we stopped being a God-fearing people. But do we become God-fearing
men by taking off our shoes? Does that ritual instill in us an

awareness of the holiness of God? Why not light small bushes
on fire too? Or hold up cigarette lighters like they do at
rock concerts? Is this account in Scripture intended to give
us a literal example to follow today? Does the passage teach
us about soles or does it really teach us about souls?

Reaching Out and Touching Someone

Admittedly, Hayford's message in 1995 was an improve-
ment on at least one message he gave in 1994 about circumcision at the Promise Keepers conference in Anaheim, California. His stated text for that conference was Genesis 17,
where God institutes circumcision as a sign and seal of the
covenant of grace entered into with Abraham (Rom. 4:11).
It was also a visible reminder that God's covenant people
were to be separate from the surrounding nations and were
to be more faithful to their covenant Lord because they,
unlike the surrounding nations, belonged to Him. Of course,
circumcision also foreshadowed the sign, seal, and visible
mark of differentiation in the new covenant: baptism (Col.
2:8-15).

But instead of teaching these important truths, Hayford
taught that God required circumcision in the Old Testament
for three reasons: (1) "God wants to touch your very identity as a man;" (2) "[God] wants to reach out and touch your
secret and private parts [which] enables Him to better perform surgery on the heart;" and (3) "God wants to touch
man's creative parts."[12]

Does God circumcise men's hearts today? Without a
doubt. But that circumcision has nothing to do with our
"identity" as men, our "secret and private parts," or our "creative parts" for that matter. Paul tells us how we ought to
apply Genesis 17 today in Colossians 2:8-15, and it isn't what
Hayford imagines. Whereas God's people were set apart from
His enemies by circumcision in the Old Testament, in the
New Testament that distinguishing mark is baptism. Whereas
the Old Testament rite of circumcision was a sign pointing

the saints of old to the Christ to come, so the New Testament rite of baptism points his people back to Him. Whereas the Old Testament rite of circumcision blessed its recipients when they owned up to the gracious covenant it signified, so the New Testament rite of baptism does likewise. And to the extent that there *is* a symbolic meaning to the act of circumcision, it is not at all "affirming" as Hayford would have us believe. Paul tells us in Colossians 2 that this circumcision is a putting off the body of the sins of the flesh (v. 11).

Properly understood, circumcision points us to Christ, not ourselves. Its focus was never on the recipient or his "secret and private parts," as Hayford would have us believe. Rather, its focus was Christ and the redemptive benefits God's people possessed in Christ as they, with types and shadows, looked forward in faith to Him and to the glorious work He would fulfill on their behalf as their Prophet, Priest, and King. In short, circumcision is about sin, not skin. It is about hearts, not parts.

Weakening the Currency

We could go on and on about how Promise Keepers speakers and writers regularly allegorize the Old Testament by telling us to look for the "Aarons and Hurs" in life so that, like Joshua, we will be able "to defeat the 'Amelakites' of [our lives] with teams of godly men."[13] Or about how *New Man* suggests, if not approves of, the view that Christ, "(w)ith a staff of 12 unlikely men," became "the most effective [chief] executive in history . . . [whose results] were second to none."[14]

But the point should be obvious by now. Promise Keepers has not made just a few isolated but unfortunate mistakes. It has counterfeited true biblical interpretation and application again and again, thereby weakening its currency in the body of Christ.

We rejoiced, then, when we recently came across an article in *New Man* instructing readers in the basics of biblical interpretation entitled, "Seven Deadly Sins of Bible Study (And How to Avoid Them)."[15] In this article, the author, Jack Kuhatschek, discusses several serious dangers of biblical interpretation: proof texting, being too literal, ignoring the Bible's background, relying on faulty translations, reading into Scripture, thinking you can do it all, and failing to apply what you learn. The irony is that Kuhatschek could have taken all of his illustrations of what not to do from what Promise Keepers has said and written. Our hope is that Kuhatschek and others will challenge Promise Keepers to do better in the days ahead since it is a dangerous thing to make the words of Scripture, in the words of Alice, mean so many different things.

But there are those out there who, when faced with Alice's challenge, may choose to respond, like Humpty, by proclaiming that the question is not whether you can make words mean so many different things, but rather, "the question is . . . which is to be master—that's all."

And that's the real issue. By making words mean what we want them to mean, we are saying that we are masters over our words. Or perhaps, it is a tacit admission that we are serving a different master altogether, whether wittingly or unwittingly. Regrettably, in the case of Promise Keepers, that master sometimes is psychology. Sometimes it is secular men's movement theory. At still other times, it is the "gospel" of works righteousness. While some submit to the one true Master, some, sadly, do not. No matter what their other master may be, we would all agree that it is both wrong and dangerous to serve a different master. Those who do, like Humpty, are eventually headed for a great fall.

[1] Wellington Boone, *SPPK*, p. 26.

[2] Anon., "Promise Keepers Fact Sheet (10/3/95)."

[3] "Raising the Standard," *New Man*, January/February, vol. 2, no. 1, 1995, p. 90, (emphasis added).

[4] *Brothers!*, p. 83, attributed to Howard G. Hendricks (emphasis added).

[5] Robert Liparulo, "The Voice That Soars," *New Man*, March/April, 1996, p. 76

[6] "Into-Me-See," *New Man*, March/April, 1995, vol. 2, no. 2, p. 42.

[7] *Ibid.*

[8] *Ibid.*

[9] Dave Branon, quoting Desmond Armstrong in "Surviving the Cut," *New Man*, March/April, 1995, vol. 2, no. 2, p. 38.

[10] "Is This Revival?" November/December, 1995, vol. 2, no. 6, pp. 22-23.

[11] *Ibid.*, p. 25.

[12] Anon., "Promise Keepers: Ecumenical 'Macho-Men' for Christ," *Biblical Discernment Ministries Letter*, p. 6, n.d.

[13] Chuck Miller, *WMAM*, pp. 130-131.

[14] Quoting James F. Hind, "Jesus as CEO?" March/April, 1995, vol. 2, no. 2, p. 18.

[15] *New Man*, January/February, 1996, vol. 3, no. 1, pp. 39-41, 43.

Part Three:
Promises, Promises

❈ EIGHT ❈

Better Not to Vow

Having noted some of the things that Promise Keepers has done well and some general causes for concern emanating from the movement and its message, we will now focus for the next few chapters on some particular concerns. These concerns arise from the now-famous seven promises which are the core commitments made by those who call themselves promise keepers. But before delving into the promises themselves, we must first pause and ask whether, and under what circumstances, it is proper for Christians to make promises when those promises, like the seven promises, amount to vows.

The Promise Keepers Platform

Political parties in our country are known by their platforms, the list of propositions that defines the party and what it intends to accomplish if its candidates are elected to office. Platforms also allow candidates to decide whether they can, in good conscience, run for office on the party's ticket. The seven promises function like a party platform, not because they are political in nature, but because they define the Promise Keepers movement and its message. They also serve to distinguish promise keepers from the rest of the pack.

To become a promise keeper, one must make seven promises. The process of becoming a promise keeper, according to Promise Keepers president, Randy Phillips, "starts by making some promises—promises we intend to keep."[1] The promises themselves are described variously by the Promise Keepers movement not only as *commitments* (". . .a Promise Keeper seizes the moment for Jesus by making commitments. Yes, commitments!"),[2] but also as *pledges* ("Lord as we enter in/We pledge to live/As godly men"),[3] *covenants* ("And as we enter in this covenant/We will seek Your holy face . . .")[4] and *vows* ("Lord we vow to live holy/Bowing our knees to You only . . .").[5] During the typical Promise Keepers conference, the process of making these vows is solemnized by some kind of ceremony or ritual, such as raising a clenched fist and echoing "Yes, Jesus" after each promise is read to affirm it before the Lord and others.

Indeed, the seven promises are vows—agreements entered into between a man and God, whereby the man explicitly or implicitly appeals to God to witness and sanction what he has promised to do. Says one observer of the Promise Keepers movement, "I praise God for the men who vow before Him to be men of integrity."[6] Yet another author, reflecting on the 1995 conference season, spoke of many renewing "vows of commitment to family and calling."[7]

Serious Business

Since the seven promises are vows, we should take time to see what Scripture has to say about vows. Many would condemn vows altogether, and on that basis, they would condemn the seven promises. While the seven promises themselves are not beyond question (as we will explore in subsequent chapters), the threshold question before us now is whether Scripture permits or forbids vows like the seven promises.

The scriptural point of departure is the third commandment, "Thou shalt not take the name of the Lord thy God in vain: for the Lord will not hold him guiltless that taketh his name in vain" (Ex. 20:7). This commandment is rich with meaning. To begin with, the phrase "the name of the Lord thy God" does not refer only to the literal name of God. Rather, *the name of God* refers comprehensively to God, including God's literal name, anything by which God makes Himself known, and ultimately, God Himself. In short, to call on the name of God is to call on God Himself.

While the name of God is used comprehensively to refer ultimately to God Himself, the phrase translated *in vain* means "falsely" (*cf.* Is. 59:4). The word translated "taketh" means "to bear" or "carry," as believers bear or carry His name when they are called *Christians*. But of course if we cannot live in a false manner under His name, still less may we speak or swear falsely in His name. So the verse bluntly excludes false oaths. "Thou shalt not swear (utter) the name of God to emptiness (vanity)." Simply put, we should refrain from appealing to the name of God to confirm or bear witness to a falsehood. When we appeal to God by means of vows, we must honor God by honoring our vows. In the eyes of God, vows are serious business.

Not Necessarily Sinful

Because vows are serious business, some Christians have taught that Scripture forbids them outright. To bolster this contention, they cite Matthew 5:33-37, wherein we find the oft-quoted command, "swear not at all." And at first blush, this passage appears to forbid all vows. But when this passage is carefully studied, it does not forbid all vows. Christ rejects only unlawful or unbiblical vows.

Like any passage, Matthew 5:31-37 must be studied in light of the general context of Scripture as a whole, which, in this case, reveals that God does not forbid all vows. In fact, God actually *commands* His people to swear by His name on certain occasions. In Deuteronomy 6:13, for example, God's people were commanded, "You shall fear only the Lord your God; and you shall worship Him, and swear by His name." Far from prohibiting all oaths and vows, Isaiah tells us that "he who swears in the earth shall swear by the name of God" (Is. 65:16). God sanctions lawful oaths and vows to such an extent that He promises to build up those who swear by His name (Jer. 12:16). Because God has commanded His people to swear by His name, He cannot forbid all oaths and vows. God does not command what He simultaneously condemns.

Scripture also teaches us that taking oaths or making vows is an act of confession and religious worship. We already saw in Deuteronomy 6:13 that God commanded His people to swear in His name precisely because swearing in God's name is one way to worship and fear Him (*cf.* Deut. 10:20). Isaiah confirms this connection between swearing and worship; when he prophesies about the Assyrians and Egyptians coming into a covenantal relationship with God, he says that they will swear in the name of God (Is. 19:18). The Swiss Reformer, John Calvin, explains that "by swearing in the Lord's name they will profess his religion."[8]

But exactly how is swearing an act of confession and worship? When we duly swear in God's name, we confess several things about God. To begin with, we confess that He exists. Moreover, we confess several of His attributes as revealed in Scripture: we testify that He is omnipresent and omniscient, that He is eternal and immutable, that He is just and true, that He is powerful and wrathful. By confessing His existence and attributes, we also confess that He is the Supreme Judge over all the earth and that we are accountable to Him for all that we do and say. Though the word of men may fail, the word of God never fails. Though men may fail, God never fails. By making vows in God's name, we confess Him to be the ultimate arbiter of truth, and we worship Him, the God of truth, in spirit and in truth (Jn. 4:24).

Scripture not only reveals that God commands His people to swear and that such swearing, if properly done, is an act of religious worship; it also commends to us those who took oaths and made vows. God Himself swears. David, anticipating the eternal priesthood of Christ exclaims under the inspiration of the Spirit, "The Lord has sworn and will not change His mind, Thou art a priest forever . . ." (Ps. 110:4). The author of Hebrews tells us that God swore not only by demonstrating that what the psalmist anticipated in Psalm 110:4 had been fulfilled in Christ (Heb. 7:21), but also when He made a covenant with Abraham: "For when God made the promise to Abraham, since He could swear by no one greater, He swore by Himself" (Heb. 6:13). God the Father undertook oaths and vows. And He never sinned by so doing. Consequently, not all vows are sinful.

What is true of God the Father is equally true with respect to God the Son. Psalm 110:4 and Hebrews 7:21 teach us that God swore that He would provide an eternal high priest (anticipation), while in Hebrews 7:21, God honored His vow by sending his Son, as our High Priest (fulfillment). The members of the triune Godhead vowed to save their people and they fulfilled that vow perfectly (Jn. 17). Thus, the life of the Son was the very fulfillment of a vow made by and with the Father. Christ also undertook an oath when questioned by Caiaphas, the high priest as recorded in the gospel of Matthew. After Christ remained silent during the accusational phase of his trial, Caiaphas charged Christ, exclaiming, "I adjure You by the living God, that You tell us whether You are the Christ, the Son of God. Jesus said to him, You have said it yourself . . ." (Matt. 26:63-64a). Literally translated, Caiaphas said to Christ "I swear You [call on you to swear]" or "I charge You." In the rabbinical form of directly affirming an oath, Christ responded to Caiaphas. In other words, by answering Caiaphas's adjuration, Christ undertook an oath that what He was saying was true. Thus, Christ took oaths. Yet we know that He never sinned (Heb. 4:15). Therefore, not all oaths and vows are sinful.

Just as Christians are commanded to imitate God the Father (Eph. 5:1), so they are commanded to imitate God the Son. "The one who says he abides in Him," writes John, "ought himself to walk in the same manner as He walked" (1 Jn. 2:6). The example of Christ teaches us that under some circumstances, we may make vows. Since the Living Word perfectly lived by the written Word, and since the Living Word swore, the written Word cannot forbid all vows.

The Word of God not only records the examples of the Father and the Son; it also records for our benefit and instruction the example of the Apostle Paul who often supported what he said with oaths: (1) "For God . . . is my witness . . ." (Rom 1:9; Phil. 1:8); (2) "But I call God as witness to my soul . . ." (2 Cor. 1:23); (3) ". . . God is witness . . ." (1 Thess. 2:5); (4) "you are witnesses, and so is God . . ." (I Thess. 2:10); and (5) "I adjure you by the Lord . . ." (1 Thess. 5:27). As you can see, there is no shortage of biblical proof that Paul swore. But the Bible doesn't record the example of Paul as a resource for our idle theological speculation. Rather, we are commanded to imitate Paul, as he, in turn, imitated Christ (1 Cor. 4:16; 11:1).

As opposed to condemning all oaths and vows, Scripture actually permits them under some circumstances. To interpret Christ as forbidding all vows is to foist a contradiction on Scripture itself, as well as on the Father, the Son, and the apostle Paul, since, on this interpretation, they all swore contrary to Scripture. The general context of Scripture, therefore, does not support the notion that Scripture forbids all vows.

Swear Not at All?

What is true of the general context of Scripture as a whole, is also true of the particular context of the Sermon on the Mount which, when properly understood, proves beyond doubt that Christ was simply correcting Pharisaical abuses of, and glosses on, the Law. In the Sermon on the Mount, Christ constantly contrasts what the ancients said about the Law (*i.e.* their glosses on the Law) with what God says about the Law (the actual requirements of the Law) by repeating the formula: "Ye have heard that it was said [glosses] . . . But I say unto you [requirements] . . ." The Pharisees, for example, taught that the Law only forbade murder; Christ taught that the Law, properly understood, also forbade hatred. The Pharisees taught that the Law only forbade adultery; Christ taught that the Law, properly understood, also forbade lust. The Pharisees taught that one was to love his neighbor and hate his enemy when the Law affirmed the former but never even taught the latter. At every juncture, Christ checks his opponents and their abuse of the Law.

Likewise, Christ corrected Pharisaical misconceptions about oaths and vows. From this passage, it appears that the Pharisees thought that one could swear as often as he wished as long as he did not do so falsely and as long as he did not swear in the literal name of God. Christ's opponents appeared to swear frequently and round-aboutly. Christ attacks both of these errors head on by showing the Pharisees that heaven, earth, Jerusalem and even their own heads have their ultimate reference point in God: heaven is the throne of God; the earth is His footstool; Jerusalem is the city of the Great King; and it is that King who controls even the hair on one's head (*cf.* Matt. 23:16-23). In other words, when they swore by heaven, they swore by the God of heaven because the universe and everything in it, to use the words of Calvin, are stamped with His glory. By swearing in these ways, the Pharisees failed to see that one still takes the name of God in vain no matter how he wishes to dress up his words.

But what does Christ mean when he says that anything more than a "yes" or "no" "cometh of evil"? Whatever He means, He cannot be forbidding all oaths and vows since they are commanded and commended elsewhere in Scripture and since both the Father and the Son, as well as the apostle Paul, undertook or made oaths and vows. Admittedly, this passage is difficult, but one possible interpretation of it may be found by understanding that in the New Testament Greek, the phrase translated "of evil" refers to the origin of oaths and vows. What Christ means is that anything beyond "yes" and "no"—an oath or a vow—has its origin in evil; in other words, oaths and vows arose as a result of evil or the Fall. It is distrust, dishonesty, and inconsistency which make vows necessary in the first place. If there were no sin, oaths and vows would be unnecessary. But just because oaths and vows are occasioned by the Fall doesn't necessarily make them evil in and of themselves. To suggest otherwise is to commit the genetic fallacy, assuming without proof that what is true of the genesis (origin) of something is true of the thing itself. After all, civil government became necessary only after the Fall (to restrain the social manifestations of sin); yet civil government is not inherently evil because of that fact. In the same way, clothing is "of evil." Hence, just because vows became necessary after the Fall as a result of evil, does not mean that vows are inherently evil. In any event, we know from the general context of Scripture that vows are not forbidden *per se*.

Biblical Guidelines for Vows

Now that we have seen that the Bible does not condemn all vows, the key issue in analyzing the process of making the seven promises is whether the promises accord with the guidelines for making oaths and vows contained in the Bible.

While the specific content of each promise will be analyzed in subsequent chapters, at this point we simply need to compare the process of making the seven promises to the following biblical principles for making vows.

1. *The Vow Must be Biblical*
One cannot bind himself to do that which Scripture forbids, since no one can bind himself to sin.

2. *The Vow Must be True*
What you are about to say must be true, or you must do what you are about to promise. "If a man makes a vow to the Lord, or takes a vow to bind himself with a binding obligation, he shall not violate his word; he shall do according to all that proceeds out of his mouth" (Num. 30:2). If, therefore, you know that you are about to utter a falsehood or you know that you have no intention of *absolutely* honoring your word, then you should not make the vow. As the Preacher in the Book of Ecclesiastes proclaims, "When you make a vow to God, do not be late in paying it, for He takes no delight in fools. Pay what you vow! It is better that you should not vow than that you should vow and not pay" (Eccl. 5:4-5).

3. *The Vow Must be Necessary*
Even if what you say is true or you intend to honor what you promise, you should not vow if vowing is unnecessary (Ex. 20:7). Scripture forbids all superfluous vows (Matt. 5:33-37; 23:16-22). There must be an adequate reason why appealing to God is necessary (*e.g.*, Ex 22:10-11). The third commandment condemns all unnecessary, colloquial, and irreverent vowing.

4. *The Vow Must be Attainable*
You must be able to attain what you have vowed, and you must be prepared to abide by your vow, no matter how

your personal interests or circumstances may change. The godly man "swears to his own hurt and does not change" (Ps. 15:4; 24:4). If you are not able, or prepared, to stand steadfastly by what you have vowed, no matter what happens, then you should not make the vow.

5. *The Vow Must Appeal to God Alone*
Scripture emphatically commands us to swear only in the name of God (Deut. 6:13; 10:20; Jer. 5:7; Zeph. 1:4-5). In no uncertain terms, God forbids swearing by other gods because swearing is an act of religious worship; when people swear by other gods, they violate the first and second commandments. God is so angered with those who swear by other "gods" that He declares that He will "cut off" those who do so (Zeph. 1:4-5). Although oaths and vows must appeal to God alone, there are a variety of ways in which one can appeal to God in the context of a vow: (1) "give glory to the God of Israel" (Josh 7:19); (2) "as the Lord lives" (Judg. 8:19; Ruth 3:13; 1 Sam 14:39; 2 Sam. 2:27; Jer. 38:16); (3) "The Lord do so to me and more also" (Ruth 1:17; 1 Sam. 14:44; 2 Sam. 3:9, 35; 1 Kings 2:23; 2 Kings 6:31); (4) "May the Lord be a true and faithful witness" (Jer. 42:5); (5) "I adjure you by the living God" (Matt. 26:63); (6) "I adjure you by the Lord" (1 Thess. 5:27); (8) "But I call God as witness to my soul" (2 Cor.1:23); (9) ". . . God is witness" (1 Thess. 2:5); (10) "You are witnesses and so is God" (1 Thess. 2:10).

6. *The Vow Must Be Clear and Unambiguous*
The language of the vow must be unequivocal and unambiguous so as to be clearly understood by all parties. The old Princeton theologian, Charles Hodge, told the story of a commander who swore to citizens of a besieged city that if they surrendered, not a drop of their blood would be shed. After securing their surrender, the commander then burned them all at the stake! We should never take oaths or make

them by means of linguistic chicanery since "all things are open and laid bare to the eyes of Him with whom we have to do" (Heb. 4:13).

Back to the Seven Promises

So how do the seven promises stack up? Let's examine them:

A Promise Keeper is committed to honoring Jesus Christ through worship, prayer, and obedience to God's Word in the power of the Holy Spirit.

A Promise Keeper is committed to pursuing vital relationships with a few other men, understanding that he needs brothers to help him keep his promises.

A Promise Keeper is committed to practicing spiritual, moral, ethical, and sexual purity.

A Promise Keeper is committed to building strong marriages and families through love, protection, and biblical values.

A Promise Keeper is committed to supporting the mission of his church by honoring and praying for his pastor, and by actively giving his time and resources.

A Promise Keeper is committed to reaching beyond any racial and denominational barriers to demonstrate the power of biblical unity.

A Promise Keeper is committed to influencing his world, being obedient to the Great Commandment (Mark 12:30-31) and the Great Commission (Matt. 28:19-20).[9]

Even a cursory glance at the seven promises reveals that, with a few exceptions, the problem is not so much with the promises themselves as it is with the applications made by those who expound them, a theme to which we shall return in subsequent chapters. But a couple of concerns arise from the fact that men are being encouraged to make these promises or vows to the Lord. To begin with, Promise Keepers has not developed a sound, biblical theology of vows; consequently, it has not properly warned men how serious it is to make vows to the Lord. Men who attend Promise Keepers conferences should not be worked up emotionally to make the seven promises, and they should know what a serious matter it is to make them. Admittedly, warning men does not make for good marketing, but true integrity demands a warning nonetheless.

Moreover, some Promise Keepers authors and speakers sound an overly triumphalistic note when it comes to the seven promises, thinking that we actually have the ability to keep the seven promises in all their rigor:

> Wives, children, churches and communities all seem to agree that what we desperately need today are men who are promise keepers: men who won't compromise the truth, men who are true to their word, men who are trustworthy. Promise Keepers is committed to igniting, equipping and uniting men to do just that—keep their promises.[10]

While we have addressed this triumphalism already as a failure to understand the law of God and the gospel of Christ, we raise it here again because it may very well be the reason men are encouraged to make the promises in the first place—because some in the Promise Keepers movement really think that men can keep them.

Other Promise Keepers spokesmen, however, frankly admit that we will stumble and fall when it comes to the seven promises. Says Randy Phillips, the president of Promise Keepers,

Those seven simple commitments take a lifetime to live out. . . . [Living out the promises] is a process, at times a struggle. . . .

[Y]ou'll have ups and downs. Sometimes you'll fail. None of us likes to fail, but it happens.[11]

While this honesty is refreshing, it is also deeply troubling, for men are being encouraged to make vows to the Lord *which they know they cannot keep*. Brian Peterson, the editor of *New Man* magazine, honestly confesses that promise keepers will fail, but he nevertheless defends making the seven promises:

Don't be afraid to commit yourself to high standards because you're tired of failing. Each of the Seven Promises of a Promise Keeper begins with "A Promise Keeper *is committed to . . .*" Commitment doesn't mean perfection. The promises reflect a devotion to a biblical standard, striving in God's strength.[12]

Peterson to the contrary, the word *commit* means "to bind or obligate, as by pledge." There is no way around it; those who affirm the seven promises are binding themselves to do them. Obligating themselves. Pledging themselves. Vowing to the Lord that they will actually do what they say. In light of this fact, hear again what the Word of God has to say:

If a man makes a vow to the Lord, or takes a vow to bind himself with a binding obligation, he shall not violate his word; he shall do according to all that proceeds out of his mouth (Num. 30:2).

As we have already seen, the Bible also tells us that we are to "pay what [we] vow!" and that it "is better that [we] should not vow than that [we] should vow and not pay" (Eccl. 5:4-5). To make a vow we cannot or do not keep is to make a false vow. It is swearing God's name to a falsehood. It is violating the third commandment, a sin of the most grievous sort.

"Where a vow is falsely taken," warns one writer, "it is a heaven-daring attempt to enlist the Almighty in the sanction of the creature's lie and is thus, either the most outrageous levity, or the most outrageous impiety of which he can be guilty."[13] It is always dangerous to engage in "heaven-daring" behavior. Lest we forget, the third commandment contains a promise, a promise of punishment for those who violate it: "the Lord will not hold him guiltless that taketh His name in vain" (Ex. 20:7). Since God will punish those who take His name in vain, we would do well to realize that it is a terrible thing to fall into the hands of the living God. Instead of invoking God's greater wrath and judgment by making false vows, we must begin to honor God in all that we do and in all that we say. We should also refrain from making unnecessary vows, and this relates to the seven promises.

But how can we ever begin to honor the name of God in all that we do and say? After all, every sin we commit is a violation of the third commandment in that we bear or carry the name of Christ as *Christians*, yet deny that name when we sin. What can we do? We can start by realizing, once again, that ultimately, the answer is not found in us. It is found only in Christ. We must own up to the only One who ever kept His promises—the One whose very life fulfilled the covenant promises made with the Father from the foundation of the universe. Christ perfectly fulfilled every vow or promise made with the Father and died in our place for all our broken vows or promises. Apart from Him and His enabling hand, we have no hope. But in Him alone, we have hope and help in time of need. May we turn from ourselves and our own supposed promise-keeping and turn instead to Him and His promise-keeping. For all the promises of God find their "yes" in Him (2 Cor. 1:20).

[1] *SPPK*, p. 8; *TPPK*, p. 2.

[2] *SPPK*, p. 8.

[3] Scott Wesley Brown and David Hampton, "Godly Men," *Raise the Standard, Promise Keepers Conference Edition for 1995.*

[4] *Ibid.*

[5] Morris, Brown, "The Family Prayer Song," *Raise the Standard Promise Keepers Conference Edition for 1995.*

[6] Diane Eble, "Reason to Rejoice," *New Man*, March/April, 1995, vol. 2, no. 2, p. 80.

[7] David Halbrook, "Is This Revival?" *New Man*, November/December, 1995, vol. 2, no. 6, p. 21.

[8] John Calvin, *Institutes of the Christian Religion*, ed. by John T. McNeil, trans. by Lewis Ford Battles, Library of Christian Classics (Philadelphia, PA: Westminster, 1960), 2.8.23.

[9] *SPPK*, pp. 13, 43, 69, 101, 129, 153, 181.

[10] "What is Promise Keepers?," *New Man*, November/December, 1994, p. 70.

[11] Introduction, *TPPK*, pp. 2-3.

[12] Brian Peterson, "The Fruit of Failing," *New Man*, July/August, 1995, vol. 3, no. 4, p. 8.

[13] R. L. Dabney, *Systematic Theology* (Edinburgh, Scotland: The Banner of Truth Trust, 1985 [1871]), p. 364.

NINE

With Fear and Trembling—Promise 1

A Promise Keeper is committed to honoring Jesus Christ through worship, prayer, and obedience to God's Word in the power of the Holy Spirit.[1]

Our relationship with God is the foundation of all other relationships. The Promise Keepers quite properly begin with a commitment of "honoring Jesus Christ through worship, prayer, and obedience to God's Word . . ." Our proper worship of God and obedience to His Word are central to our lives.

A Way that Seems Right

Given the central role of worship in the life of the believer, we must be very clear in our minds how God is acceptably worshipped. Throughout Scripture, we see men approaching God in a way that seemed to them a good idea at the time, but the results were disastrous. Cain was not accepted in his offering to God (Gen. 4:4-5); Nadab and Abihu were struck down by God for offering strange incense (Lev. 10:1-2); King Uzziah was struck with leprosy for worshipping God contrary to His Word (2 Chron. 26:16-20). The list could easily be multiplied, but the idea is clear: how God is to be worshipped must be defined by Him, not by His worshippers.

Promise Keepers author, Jack Hayford, makes this same point when he writes that God

> demands attention to *His* ways of worship. The whimsy and flimsy of human reason, the puff and pride of human arrogance, only need to pass once through the flame of His presence to be shown for what they are: *Nothing*.[2]

Shortly after Hayford's chapter, the editor of *Seven Promises of a Promise Keeper* asks readers whether they are "involved in worshipping God according to the biblical pattern."[3]

All this is fine and good. We should not worship God according to what *seems* right to us, but only what *is* right to Him. In short, we must worship according to the biblical pattern. But where do we find that pattern? Hayford thinks that we should look within our own hearts:

> Listen to Jesus' words: "Blessed are the pure in heart, for they will see God" (Matt. 5:8). Check this closely, because too many read this text to mean, "Everybody who's perfect will arrive in heaven some day." But Jesus wasn't talking about purity in ritual terms. He was talking about the fundamental definition: *Purity* is "that which is undiluted by other substances." Now, join that to the place Jesus pointed at, the *heart* of a man—*that's* where God seeks undiluted commitment.
>
> So what does it all mean? The answer is in what Jesus did and didn't say. He *didn't* say, "Blessed are the pure in mouth . . . hands . . . mind . . . feet." No. Christ calls you and me to come, candidly and with a *heart fully opened* in worship, into the privacy of His presence. Then something will happen: If we bring our whole heart, without restriction or reservation, we will see God![4]

For Hayford, worshipping according to the biblical pattern requires that we bring our "whole heart" to God, despite the fact that the Bible tells us quite frankly that the human heart is "deceitful above all things and desperately wicked: who can know it?" (Jer. 17:9). And the fact that a man is a Christian does not necessarily make his heart a reliable guide. The apostle Paul says at one point that his conscience was clear, but that this did not necessarily mean anything. In the best saints, the flesh wars against the Spirit. The bottom line is that if we could purify our deceitfully wicked hearts on our own, we wouldn't need a Savior to purify them for us. Because the human heart is not naturally good, it cannot be where we turn to find the biblical pattern for anything, let alone worship.

As with Hayford, far too many evangelicals today are too quick to turn within, to their hearts or feelings, to determine what is pleasing to God in worship. As opposed to looking within, one Promise Keeper writer quite correctly tells us exactly where we need to look: God "speaks through His Word, not through our feelings. . . ."[5]

Thinking God's Thoughts

Besides, where did we ever get the idea that what *we* think pleases God really pleases Him? One of the indications of the sinfulness of the human heart is our ability to be man-centered in the midst of the most God-centered thing we do—worship. C. S. Lewis made an observation which addresses the heart of this problem.

> I read in a periodical the other day that the fundamental thing is how we think of God. By God Himself, it is not! How God thinks of us is not only more important, but infinitely more important. Indeed, how we think of Him is of no importance except in so far as it is related to how He thinks of us.[6]

We like to evaluate worship services in the car on the way home from church. This is proper and acceptable—but do we discuss whether *God* was pleased with us, or whether *we* were pleased? It may seem like nit-picking, but the difference between these two modes of thought is as great as the difference between the geocentric view of the solar system before Copernicus and the heliocentric view which came after.

As we worship, is the audience God or man? Too many Christians treat their worship of God (as seen, for example, in the way they select a church) in the same way they select a gas station or a department store. If they like this or that, they go. If they do not like it, then they go elsewhere. But the real question is not what we like, but what God "likes" and how we can know.

Granted, Promise Keepers does not claim to be a church. Nor does it claim to be conducting renegade worship services. Promise Keepers is a parachurch organization, that is, it is self-consciously operating "alongside" the church. But because Promise Keepers is such a large organization, its patterns of worship will certainly affect the patterns of worship in the churches from which its men come. Consequently, it is worthwhile to look at the patterns of worship at a typical Promise Keepers conference, and ask whether they are scriptural.

We must remember Promise 5 ("A Promise Keeper is committed to supporting the mission of his church by honoring and praying for his pastor, and by actively giving his time and resources"). Pastors will plainly tell anyone who asks that men do not come back from a Promise Keepers conference unaffected. One of the goals of Promise Keepers is to revitalize men in order to revitalize them in their involvement with the church. This means that men will come back from Promise Keepers with certain ideas about worship in their home churches. In many cases, their home worship will already be like that of Promise Keepers, but in other situations, it will be dissimilar—and quite possibly perceived as "dead" because it is not lively in the same way the rally was. This fact raises two concerns. The first is the means of our worship, and the second is the manner of our worship.

Means and Manners

The Bible actually has quite a bit to say about the means of worship. If we are going to worship according to the biblical pattern in the local church, our worship should consist of things like calling the congregation to worship and offering a benediction (Num. 6:21-27; Rom. 1:7; 15:33; 1 Cor. 1:3; 16:23-24; 2 Cor. 13:14); praying (Acts 2:42; Eph. 5:20; Phil. 4:6; 1 Thess. 5:17); reading the Word of God (2 Thess. 3:14; 1 Cor. 14:37; Col. 4:16; 2 Pet. 3:15); preaching, teaching, and hearing the Word of God (Acts 2:42; 20:7-12; 1 Cor. 14:26; Col. 3:16; 2 Tim. 4:2; Rom. 10:17); administering the ordinances of baptism and the Lord's Supper (Matt. 28:19; Lk. 22:14-20; Acts 2:42; 1 Cor. 11:17-34); giving and receiving tithes and offerings to support God's work and the care of the poor (1 Cor. 16:1-2); and singing praises (Ps. 47:7; Eph. 5:19; Col. 3:16). And if the Bible is really our pattern of worship, we will not try to offer "strange" or "unauthorized fire" to the Lord, as did Nadab and Abihu, who paid dearly for their presumptuousness (Lev. 10:1-2; Num. 3:4). They learned first-hand that their God was a consuming fire! At all times, we would do well to remember that He is the Creator and we are His creatures, and that He grants us the privilege of worshipping Him on *His* terms.

But it is not enough if we get a fix on the proper means of worshipping God. True worship not only requires that we approach God with the right means, but also that we do so in the right manner. With regard to the manner of worship, an area of grave concern is the irreverence that has come to permeate the thinking of modern evangelicalism in the late-twentieth century. For example, popular writer and

Promise Keepers speaker, Stu Weber, recently had this to say in *Locking Arms*, in a chapter entitled "History's Greatest High Five."

> If there were high fives in the first century, I can think of a couple of scenes where Jesus likely would have practiced them. In fact, in one of those scenes His arms actually were extended, though not over His head. But His shout was a victory shout. It was a shout of great pressure and great pleasure (see Isaiah 53:11). There on the cross, when He had paid the price for our sins, with arms fully extended, the Lord of the universe shouted, "It is finished!" It was the greatest arms-extended, high-five moment in history![7]

As the quotation makes clear, Weber is a sincere Christian who seeks to glory in the death of Christ. At the same time, however, it is equally clear that, with regard to appropriate reverence on a subject such as this, he is completely tone-deaf. The sacrifice of Christ for the sins of His people topped off with a "high-five"? Why not have the Lord moonwalk off the set, stage left?

This is not leveled at Weber as a personal criticism. The church at large has created a climate where informality and spontaneity are greatly prized in spiritual things. We must not be surprised at the results. This climate is characteristic of Promise Keeper events. When, at the rallies, the two sides of the stadium roar back and forth, "We love Jesus, yes, we do. We love Jesus, how 'bout you!" the effect is to treat holy and spiritual things as though they were on the same level as the ruckus of a football game. The problem is not noise, but demeanor. The effect was very different one time when Moses "filled a stadium." He placed the people of Israel on two mountains, and had them respond with a thunderous roar to holy requirements of the covenant law of God.

> And Moses commanded the people on the same day, saying, "These shall stand on Mount Gerizim to bless the

people, when you have crossed over the Jordan: Simeon, Levi, Judah, Issachar, Joseph, and Benjamin; and these shall stand on Mount Ebal to curse: Reuben, Gad, Asher, Zebulun, Dan, and Naphtali. And the Levites shall speak with a loud voice and say to all the men of Israel: 'Cursed is the one who makes a carved or molded image, an abomination to the Lord, the work of the hands of the craftsman, and sets it up in secret.' And all the people shall answer and say, 'Amen!'" (Dt. 27:11-15).

Our motive for all that we do is to glorify God—even if it is something as mundane as eating or drinking (1 Cor. 10:31). How much more, then, should we be seeking the glory of God when we are in the act of worshipping Him? Certainly, most Christians would agree that our motive in worship should be to glorify God—but is there a snare? Yes, when we assume that whatever *we* like is suitable as an offering to God. This was the error of Cain, of Nadab and Abihu, of Uzziah, and of those guilty of "self-imposed religion" in Colossians 2:23. How do we know what glorifies God? We must seek to answer the question through Bible study. Our motive, therefore, must be to glorify God in our worship, including our singing, and we do so only when we adhere to the pattern found in His Word.

Off Pitch

Admittedly, music is just a part of our worship, but it is a very revealing part. This is because many Christians have strong feelings about their tastes in music, and we can readily see how their tastes govern what they believe is appropriate to offer to God. Music does not stand alone as a separate entity. Men express themselves to God through music. Trite and irreverent music is therefore more than unfortunate; it is an unfortunate revelation, a revelation of hearts. This is why it is important for those who sing (whether individually or together with others) to have hearts prepared to offer the sacrifice of praise. "Therefore by Him let us continually offer the sacrifice of praise to God, that is, the fruit of our lips, giving thanks to His name" (Heb. 13:15).

If we do not prepare ourselves for worship, God is not pleased with our musical offerings.

> I hate, I despise your feast days, and I do not savor your sacred assemblies. Though you offer Me burnt offerings and your grain offerings, I will not accept them, nor will I regard your fattened peace offerings. Take away from me the noise of your songs, for I will not hear the melody of your stringed instruments. But let justice run down like water, and righteousness like a mighty stream (Amos 5:21-24).

We must note this passage carefully—God evaluates worship services. And He takes a dim view of musical hypocrites.

As Christian men sing, certain characteristics should be obvious to all who hear the singing. The singing should be *reverent.* The flippancy with which some address God is truly frightening. "The Lord reigns; let the peoples tremble! He dwells between the cherubim; let the earth be moved! The Lord is great in Zion, and He is high above all the peoples. Let them praise your great and awesome name—He is holy" (Ps. 99:1-3). The KJV translation of *awesome* is not far off the mark: *terrible.* His name should instill in us a sense of reverential awe, a holy terror. We are to be a God-fearing people even as we worship Him. Moreover, this requirement to be God-fearing was not an "Old Covenant thing"—notice Paul's teaching in Philippians—"work out your own salvation with fear and trembling" (2:12). A reformation among men will not happen if they do little more than entertain jolly thoughts.

This means that what we present to God must be well-done. Beautiful and appropriate music exists. What is beautiful is not simply a matter of personal tastes. The Scripture says, "Play *skillfully* with a shout of joy . . ." (Ps. 33:3). In Colossians 3:16, we are required to have the word of Christ dwell in us richly, and the result of this is to be musical: "psalms, hymns, and spiritual songs." The music that comes forth should reflect the richness of the faith, not its poverty. If the faith is rich, then the music will be rich as well. Scripture teaches a correspondence between tree and fruit, fountain and water. In contrast, the music of Promise Keeper events is not always in keeping with remembering the holy awe we must have when we are privileged to sing before the Lord of hosts.

Yes, That's the Book for Me

Not only must our worship conform to biblical patterns, so must all that we believe and do. Promise 1 tells us that we must not only honor Christ through worship but also by "obedience to God's Word." In order to do that, we must understand how foundational God's Word is for everything. Consistent with the historic Christian creeds and confession, more than one Promise Keepers writer has written "The Bible is the final rule of faith and practice for a Christian."[8]

However, other Promise Keepers speakers and writers, though perhaps giving lip service to the sufficiency and authority of Scripture, end up diluting the biblical message with a vast array of admixtures. Case in point: Bill McCartney, the founder of Promise Keepers, once claimed that God told him, "You can fill that stadium, but if men of other races aren't there [in greater numbers], then I won't be there, either."[9] At one Promise Keepers conference in 1995, McCartney told of how some in the organization confronted him after this supposed prophesy by pointing out to him that where two or three are gathered in God's name, He is in there in the midst of them, regardless of the racial mix (Matt. 18:20).

Instead of recognizing his grievous error in presuming to speak for God contrary to His Word, McCartney refused to budge. To this day, he still goes around the country repeating what God allegedly told him and claiming to be in the right. He still apparently believes that God is an affirmative-action God who conditions His presence and blessing on racial quotas. For McCartney, Matthew 18:20 might as well read, "Where two or three are gathered in my name, and two of them are people of color, there I am in the midst of them." Contrary to McCartney, "(t)here is neither Jew nor Greek, there is neither slave nor free man, there is neither male nor female; for you are all one in Christ Jesus . . ." (Gal. 3:28). God is not a "respecter of persons" (Acts 10:34), and has clearly told us so in His Word. He is also the one who "changeth not," the One who is "the same yesterday, and today, and forever" (Mal. 3:6; Heb. 13:8).

No matter what you believe about the continuing validity of the supernatural spiritual gifts, we are told to "test the spirits to see whether they are from God" (1 Jn. 4:1). In this instance, McCartney has failed the test. His supposed prophesy was wrong, and his refusal to recant to this day is not consistent with the Promise Keepers' call to integrity.

And what a mixed message it sends to the church! "A Promise Keeper is committed to honoring Jesus Christ through . . . obedience to God's Word *except when his gut tells him otherwise.*" Perhaps McCartney should re-read his own book, *What Makes a Man?*, in which a fellow contributor correctly points out that God "speaks through His Word, not through our feelings. . . ."[10]

Another apparently innocuous but harmful example of denying the sufficiency and authority of the Bible is found in a *New Man* article written by Lee Strobel, a teaching pastor at Willow Creek Community Church near Chicago. In his popular book, *What Jesus Would Say* (Zondervan, 1995), Strobel invites his readers to imagine what Jesus would say if he conversed with some of the icons of American popular culture such as Madonna, Rush Limbaugh, and Michael Jordan. Predictably, *New Man* excerpted the chapter devoted to the imaginary encounter between Christ and Jordan. What could be more harmless, right? Wrong!

The whole idea of creating a dialogue involving Christ suffers from one fatal flaw: it puts words in Christ's mouth—quotation marks and all. No matter how you slice it, creating dialogues involving Christ adds to the Bible. It assumes in effect that the Bible hasn't said enough, that it somehow needs to be supplemented by man, and that man can do so accurately. This is dangerous. It is also unbiblical. We are not to add to, or delete from, the Word of God (Deut. 4:2; Rev. 21:18-19).

The Bible teaches us that though God "spoke long ago to the fathers in the prophets in many portions and in many ways," yet "in these last days [He] has spoken to us in His Son . . ." (Heb. 1:1-2). Christ—the Word (Jn. 1:1)—is the revelation of the Father. We don't need to speculate about what He might say to Jordan or anyone else for that matter. He has already said all He wants us to hear and read, and He has done so in His Word, the Bible. Rather than speculating about what Jesus might say, why not simply proclaim what He has said already? As opposed to imagining what His words might be, why not go to the Word itself?

The point of our concern is not that this article was specifically written to undermine biblical authority. The point is that by sanctioning this article, Promise Keepers has sent a rather dangerous message to the readers of *New Man*: namely, that it's okay to speculate about what Christ might say when He has fully and finally spoken to us already in His Word.

The Reformers were right on the mark when they taught that we are to speak where Scripture speaks and to remain silent where Scripture is silent. If we took their advice, we would be guaranteed of at least one thing: there certainly would be a lot less clamor in the church today.

Other examples of denying the sufficiency and authority of the Bible could be multiplied, but that is the whole point of this book: taking what the Promise Keepers say to the Word of God. And you shouldn't take our word for it, either. Go to the Word, as did the "noble-minded" Bereans who took even what the apostle Paul taught to the Scriptures to see whether the things he taught were true (Acts 17:11). Shouldn't we all do that? Our Sunday school children have long sung of how they "stand alone on the Word of God, the B-I-B-L-E." Promise Keepers would benefit by reading from the same page.

We Don't Need No Education

The attitude of McCartney & Co. is not an isolated occurrence within the Promise Keepers movement. There is an anti-authoritarian streak that is revealed from time to time. As just one example, consider the following lyrics to a Promise Keepers "song of encouragement":

> God doesn't need an orator
> Who knows just what to say
> He doesn't need authorities
> To reason Him away
> He doesn't need an army
> To guarantee a win
> He just needs a few good men.[11]

The rock group, Pink Floyd, cut a song some years ago which bears some vague resemblance to this song of "encouragement." The lyrics to the Pink Floyd song go like this:

> We don't need no education.
> We don't need no thought control
> No dark sarcasm in the classroom
> Teachers leave the kids alone

Hey, teacher leave us kids alone
All in all it's just another brick in the wall.
All in all you're just another brick in the wall.[12]

Just as Pink Floyd had no use for educators to teach the children entrusted to them, so Promise Keepers apparently has no use for ordained heralds of the Word of God to teach those entrusted to them. Letting the Holy Spirit move spontaneously in us is somehow preferable to a reasoned and cogent presentation of the truth by those who know "what to say." The assumption lurking behind Pink Floyd's rebellious lyrics was "We are just fine the way we are, thank you, and we don't need what you stuffed-shirt educators are trying to teach us. So there!" Sure, the Promise Keepers lyrics are a bit more diplomatic, but they are equally anti-authoritarian. In the 1960's and 1970's we called this attitude rebellion. Today, we call it evangelicalism. Boy, how times have changed!

A Mess of Pottage

Even worse, many evangelicals fail to see that the type of anti-authoritarianism fostered by Promise Keepers collapses on itself. "In the name of tearing down authoritarian walls," maintains one critic, "Promise Keepers has set itself up as an unassailable authority."[13] And Promise Keepers pays a high price for its anti-authoritarianism. Thinking it is teaching the Word of God, Promise Keepers often ends up borrowing uncritically from extra-biblical sources, baptizing those sources with a "Christian" vocabulary, and then teaching those sources as gospel truth. We have already noted how Promise Keepers has done so with psychology. Yet it also has done the same thing with the secular men's movement. And this wholesale borrowing of men's movement theory is not limited to Robert Hicks's *The Masculine Jour-*

ney. It pervades the entire Promise Keepers movement. As one renowned expert on the men's movement recently put it:

> But for all their [Promise Keepers] derision of the contemporary men's movements, they owe much of their success to those movements. To profeminists, they owe the foundational idea that men have not been good, safe partners. Men have been adversely affected by pornography and sexual fantasies. Men have not been trustworthy, and men spend too much time at work and not enough time with their families . . . .
>
> From men's rights advocates, they take the message that fatherless homes are bad and that good fathering is the single most important cure for the contemporary cultural crisis. They also draw on the men's rights suspicion of the feminist agenda; sometimes they quote Farrell directly . . . .
>
> From mythopoetics, the Promise Keepers take the theme that men have a spiritual deficit that needs to be filled, and that men are deeply wounded in the course of becoming a man. They borrow the theme that men are best able to help men to become men and that warrior men are what we need. The Promise Keepers gatherings are for men only precisely on such grounds.
>
> Had these ideas not been put forth by the various components of the men's movement, it is unlikely that such an immediate appeal to men would have been possible.[14]

Promise Keepers cannot afford to be anti-authoritarian if it wants to be biblical. If it continues this anti-authoritarianism much longer, it will end up completely selling its birthright for a mess of secular pottage. Promise Keepers speaker and writer, Wellington Boone, was so right when he wrote:

> An alarm is sounding throughout the body of Christ. It warns of impending judgment on those who do not sub-

scribe to the Word of God as the gauge for measuring all programs and philosophies.[15]

Has Promise Keepers heard this alarm yet?

---

[1] *SPPK*, pp. 8, 13.

[2] *Ibid.*, p. 18.

[3] *Ibid.*, p. 41.

[4] *Ibid.*, p. 22.

[5] Udo Middleman, *WMAM*, p. 200.

[6] C. S. Lewis, *The Weight of Glory* (Grand Rapids, MI: Eerdmans, 1965), p. 10.

[7] Stu Weber, *Locking Arms* (Portland, OR: Multnomah Books, 1995), p. 112.

[8] Patrick Morley, *New Man*, March/April, 1995, pp. 50-51.

[9] *SPPK*, p. 160.

[10] Udo Middleman, p. 200.

[11] *Songs of Encouragement for Men of Integrity*, 1994.

[12] "Another Brick In The Wall Part II," *The Wall*, 1979. Music by Pink Floyd; lyrics by Roger Waters.

[13] Michael Horton, *The Whitehorse Inn*, "What About The Promise Keepers Movement?" CURE: Anaheim, California, 1995.

[14] Kenneth Clatterbaugh, *M.E.N. Magazine*, "Whose Keepers, What Promises?," October, 1995.

[15] *WMAM*, p. 188.

❖ TEN ❖

Being a Guy's Guy—Promise 2

A Promise Keeper is committed to pursuing vital relationships with a few other men, understanding that he needs brothers to help him keep his promises.[1]

After stressing the primacy of a man's relationship with his God and His Word in Promise 1, we are told in Promise 2 that if we would be Promise Keepers we should pursue vital relationships with other Christian men.

The mission statement of the Promise Keepers affirms that "Promise Keepers is committed to unite men through vital relationships to become godly influences in their world." The editor of *Seven Promises of a Promise Keeper*, has written "[s]uch a big commitment as we have made in Promise 1—to honor Jesus Christ through worship, prayer, and obedience to His Word—cannot be fulfilled alone." But instead of pointing us to Christ and the indwelling power of the Holy Spirit, as we would expect, he instead goes on to write:

> We need like-minded friends. . . .
> God never intended for us to do it alone. . . . The concept of those who are more mature helping those who are less mature is called *mentoring*. . . . [W]e all need mentors.[2]

Why? Because "the mentor empowers the protege so they

succeed."[3] No one would deny that undergirding Promise 2 are the important biblical principles that "two are better than one" (Eccl. 4:9) and that "iron sharpens iron" (Prov. 27:17). There is something altogether necessary about admonishing, supporting, encouraging, and fellowshipping with one another in the body of Christ. After all, no man is an island. And if this is all Promise 2 is about, then it is right on target. However . . .

The "Mentorship Mandate"

When we dig a little deeper, we soon discover that there is more to Promise 2 than first meets the eye. For starters, we are told that the Bible *mandates* mentorship. This mandate is implicit in Promise 2 itself, when it states that we *need* brothers to help us keep our promises. But Promise Keepers authors themselves make the mandate implicit in Promise 2 explicit by claiming that we cannot be all that God has called us to be unless we first are united with other men in "vital relationships" through which we can become godly influences in the world.

E. Glenn Wagner, the Vice President of Ministry Advancement for the Promise Keepers, speaks explicitly of the "biblical *mandate* to develop man-to-man friendships . . ."[4] He mandates such relationships by writing, "We can and *should* develop strong mentoring relationships [with other men]."[5] *"(Y)ou haven't lived as a Christian,"* proclaims Promise Keepers author and speaker Howard G. Hendricks, *"until you have been mentored.* And you haven't known fulfillment until you have been involved in the process of mentoring."[6] Wagner puts the same point this way: "It is *impossible* for men to fulfill the commands of Scripture without being in significant relationships with one another."[7] Elsewhere, Hendricks, with his son, has written, that the "vital relationships" spoken of in Promise 2 are "relationships apart from which a man cannot live and *grow*, spiritually speaking. He *must* have those relationships to stay alive and thrive."[8] Another author confesses that he learned the hard way that

> we can't walk through life solo. Being a man of God is a "team sport." I believe that a part of our Christian walk is saddling up with a few other men and walking through life together. . .
>
> If you wish to shield yourself from Satan's poisoned-tipped arrows, you *should* cling to God's Word—and link up with other men of God. We *must* all link up for the sake of our families and our culture.[9]

No less than the president of Promise Keepers, Randy Phillips, concurs by writing that "if you want to become all God wants you to be, you *need* at least one other Christian brother to help you get there."[10] In the same vein, Geoff Gorsuch and Dan Schaffer have claimed in a Promise Keepers small group discussion guide that forming an "accountability" group is the key to maturing in Christ as men: "the *key* to their maturity in Christ is to find men of like heart and to grow—to struggle!—with them."[11]

Apparently, God overlooked this "mentorship mandate" when He only made Eve as Adam's helper and proclaimed that she was the one who was "suitable" for him—the one who would complement him in every respect and help him fulfill the commands entrusted to him in the Garden (Gen. 2:18). On the logic of the mentorship mandate, however, Adam was handicapped from the start since, apart from other men, he never could have fulfilled the commands entrusted to him at the dawn of creation.

Contrary to God's design for wives to play a unique role in helping their husbands accomplish all that God has called them to accomplish even after the Fall (Gen. 2:18, 20-22; 1 Cor. 11:8-9; Eph. 5:22-33; 1 Tim. 2:13), Wagner actually faults men for desiring to be intimate with their wives:

"Many men do desire to share their deepest feelings—but mostly with a *woman* they admire rather than another man in a mentoring relationship."[12] The mentorship mandate thus detracts from the intimacy between husband and wife that is to characterize the marital union by directing that intimacy elsewhere—to other men.

And this advice does not find its origin in the Bible. It finds its origin in secular men's movement theory. As we have already seen, the author of *Contemporary Perspectives on Masculinity* has traced this advice to its true source:

> From mythopoetics, the Promise Keepers take the theme that men have a spiritual deficit that needs to be filled, and that men are deeply wounded in the course of becoming a man. *They borrow the theme that men are best able to help men to become men* and that warrior men are what we need. The Promise Keepers gatherings are for men only precisely on such grounds.[13]

True Confessions

Redirecting marital intimacy to other men is bad enough, but another Promise Keepers author, Gregg Lewis, is a bit more blunt when he asks, point blank: "Do you have someone *other than* your wife with whom you can share your secret temptations and failures?"[14] To be sure, the phrase "other than" is a little slippery. It can mean either *in addition to your wife* or *instead of your wife*. But, from the context, it is clear that Lewis is encouraging his readers to find someone *instead of their wives* since he thereafter commends to us the example of one promise keeper (Kurt) who salved his conscience by telling his "soulmate" (Stan) instead of His wife about some sexual infidelity or other he had committed:

When things have been going well for a few weeks and then I slip up, it's easy to think, *I don't really need to bring that up*. That happened to me not long ago. And that evening after I'd met with Stan in the morning, I picked up my Bible and was reading in Psalm 32: "Blessed is the man whose sin the LORD does not count against him. . . . Blessed is he whose transgressions are forgiven . . . and in whose spirit there is no deceit." That hit me right between the eyes. But it went on to say, "When I kept silent my bones wasted away. . . . I will confess my transgressions to the LORD—and you forgave the guilt of my sin." And it was like *wow*. I had to call Stan right away and say, "Here's where I am. I messed up. Here's what happened . . ."[15]

Note that Kurt is somewhat confused. He begins by confusing confession to *God* in Psalm 32 with confession to *Stan*. In Psalm 32, David laments his grievous sin and his ensuing silence about it—that is, his failure to seek forgiveness from the Lord:

> When I kept silent about my sin, my body wasted away through my groaning all day long. For day and night *Thy* hand was heavy upon me . . . . I acknowledged my sin to *Thee*, and my iniquity I did not hide; I said, "I will confess my transgressions *to the LORD*"; and *Thou* didst forgive the guilt of my sin (vv. 3-5, emphasis added).

It is hard to imagine how Kurt could have missed the obvious: Psalm 32, from beginning to end, is a prayer to the Lord. If Kurt is going to find biblical support for confessing one of his frequent falls to Stan, he must look elsewhere in Scripture (*e.g.*, James 5:16), since Psalm 32 provides no such support.

In addition to wrongly pressing Psalm 32 into service, Kurt also appears to be more than a little confused about his biblical responsibility to make things right with his wife by confessing sins he has committed against her to her. Kurt's sexual sin was not against Stan at all. And it was not just against the Lord. It was against the Lord and, on another important level, against his wife. Yet we do not learn until much later that Kurt confessed his sin against his wife *to her*. Instead, he attempted to salve his conscience for quite some time by making confession to Stan a substitute for confessing to his wife. While he is certainly free to confess to his wife *and* Stan, he is not free to choose confessing to Stan *instead of* his wife.

This advice is not an isolated occurrence in Promise Keepers literature. It is a pervasive theme. For example, *New Man* featured an article entitled "Sex under Control" by Archibald Hart, Dean of the Graduate School of Psychology at Fuller Theological Seminary. In this article, Hart writes that after admitting that they have a problem and seeking forgiveness from the Lord, men who struggle with sexual "addiction" should follow eight steps. Of those eight steps, three involve finding a trusted "friend" who will hold the struggler accountable. This "friend" is not the man's wife; in fact, nowhere is the man's wife even mentioned in the eight-step "recovery" plan outlined by Hart. As opposed to the man's wife, the "friend" Hart encourages his readers to find is another guy: "Ask somebody to keep you accountable. Discuss your progress with *him* regularly, and give *him* permission to ask you tough questions."[16] By encouraging men to find another man to whom they can confess their sexual lapses and who will hold them accountable, Hart has bypassed the most trusted friend a man should have: his wife. Yet another *New Man* author said the same thing when he wrote that the sexual rituals committed by addicts "should be confessed to a person or group who can help a man set new boundaries and accountability."[17]

Another Promise Keepers writer, Jerry Kirk, has made the same mistake of encouraging confession to other men instead of one's wife by going as far as listing factors to help husbands decide on a case-by-case basis whether they should make specific confession of sexual infidelities to their wives:

> Any decision about confessing a sexual sin to one's wife should be made in light of these questions:
>
> • How would I feel if she were confessing these things to me?
> • Have we shown grace to each other in smaller failures?
> • Are my humility and repentance genuine? Am I following the biblical model of real confession and asking for forgiveness? ("Will you forgive me? I know I don't deserve it, but I'm asking for it.")
> • How much detail is necessary to reveal so my confession is real and her forgiveness can be complete? (Details are likely to stick painfully in her mind.)
> • Is the timing right? Do we have unhurried time to listen and talk through the issues.[18]

Like a judge faced with a complex dispute for which there is no clear legal guidance, husbands are supposed to decide whether to confess their infidelities to their wives on a case-by-case basis using the factors articulated by Kirk. But when it comes to confessing to the guys, Kirk has no reservations at all. Without skipping a beat, he turns right around and claims that there is *"(n)o substitute for personal accountability with other godly men."*[19] "We need to surround ourselves with a few men," we are told, so that we can "acknowledge" our "secret sins."[20] Put differently, husbands need to take time to decide whether or not they should confess sins against their wives to their wives, but they shouldn't hesitate for a single moment to confess their "secret sins" to the guys.

Well-intentioned though this guy-friendly advice may be, it is anything but biblical. A husband who commits any kind of sexual infidelity cannot make it right with God until he also makes it right with his wife. The two are tied together. *Any* sexual infidelity is always a covenantal sin against his wife. In Promise Keepers' jargon, it is a broken promise. Fortunately, readers of Promise Keepers literature sometimes know better than the authors themselves. One particularly adept reader of *New Man*, for example, wrote about the long road he and his wife had traveled together in overcoming his problem with pornography:

> I got help *by first admitting to my unsuspecting wife* about my secret life. This was very hard for both of us, but getting the problem into the light was critical. After that *we* shared with trusted friends and our pastor, and then got counseling . . .[21]

An anonymous author of an article in *New Man* spoke about his life as a "former adulterer" and encouraged men caught in the web of sexual infidelity to confess their sin to their wives,[22] and another author holds up pastors who confess sexual temptations to their wives as an example for his readers to follow.[23] At least some folks are doing their homework! But the vast majority of Promise Keepers writers on this subject are not.

Tipping the Scales

In addition to this problem of confession, Promise Keepers literature also encourages men to develop relationships with other men in a way that is simply imbalanced.

Constantly, Promise Keepers encourages us to ask ourselves whether we have any other men we can count on when "life happens." If not, we are warned by Gorsuch and Schaffer that we may be "caught in relational patterns that allow [us] to function but not to grow in Christ."[24] Some pretty strong words. Gorsuch and Schaffer have assumed that unless you develop the "relational patterns" encouraged by Promise Keepers, you run the risk of failing to grow in Christ. Imagine how impoverished the saints of old must have been without the benefit of this late-twentieth century wisdom!

Having simply assumed that our spiritual growth will be stunted unless we are in vital relationship with at least one other man, Gorsuch and Schaffer then give us a list of questions to test whether we have such a relationship:

- When things go badly, whom do you talk to?
- Who can you be totally honest with?
- Who is your sounding board?
- Who would you take advice from?
- When you fail, who will stand by you?
- Who do you face life's struggles with?
- Who is your confidant?
- Who holds you accountable?[25]

Presumably, we are supposed to supply the name of at least one male friend at this point, and our inability to do so somehow constitutes proof positive of our spiritual/relational impoverishment. But is this right? Read the questions again. If you cannot name your wife in response to each question, then your marriage is in real trouble. While married men should never allow themselves to develop an intimate relationship with women other than their own wives, the Bible proposes something even more radical: men should not have a more intimate relationship *with any man* as a substitute for developing such intimacy with their wives. The intimacy illustrated by each question should be preserved for your wife in marriage. And it should not need to be said, but the tenor of our times requires it. Men can fall into sexual sin with other men as well as with other women.

If you want to build on your intimacy with your wife by developing a close friendship with another man, that is one thing. If you seek to develop a close friendship with another man instead of with your wife, that is another matter entirely. *Supplementing* your marital relationship is one thing; *supplanting* it is quite another. Promise Keepers literature requires the latter. When talking about the confusion and isolation of the American male, Gorsuch and Schaffer offer their solution: God's "method is men."[26] If a brother is struggling with burnout, depression, and wounding,

> There is only one cure for this depth of isolation—a lot of time, patience, and understanding by some brothers. The wounded man is most helped by a brother's prayers and silent attention to his physical and psychological needs. Who else but a brother would do that?[27]

The only cure? How about the man's wife? His pastor and elders? His brothers *and* sisters in the body of Christ? While brothers play a vital role in the body of Christ, they do not play the only role. Nor are they necessarily to play the primary role. By applying Promise 2 in this way, Promise Keepers has undermined the marital relationship in a very serious way. It has also undermined the role of the local church, a theme we shall return to in chapter 13.

O Brother!

Still other problems plague Promise 2 as it is applied by Promise Keepers. In *Brothers!* Gorsuch and Schaffer tell us that becoming a true brother by affiliating with a group of men "represents the next phase of our commitment to Christ." This claim is made in light of the "fact" that the word *brother* replaced the word *disciple* in the New Testament.[28] Yet we do not become a brother by joining a small group study. Nor is there any proof that the word *brother* replaced the word disciple, or even if it did, that the word *brother* therefore represents a higher level of Christian commitment. After all, the word *Christian* also "replaced" the word *disciple* ("and the disciples were first called Christians at Antioch"—Acts 11:27). With the same logic, are we therefore to infer that becoming a Christian represents some subsequent phase of commitment since it, too, "replaced" the word *disciple* as a description of believers in the New Testament?

To imply that becoming a brother represents a subsequent point of commitment to Christ or to one another is simply wrong. It is also wrong to imply that we become a brother by something *we do*. We are not Christians by grace and brothers by works. By grace, we become Christians and brothers at the same time and in the same way—when God adopts us into His family. And there can be no brother-to-brother fellowship with those who reject the gospel of Christ. The question is not *when* we will become brothers but *whether* we already are brothers, and if so, *what kind* of brothers we already are and what kind of brothers we should become.

And what kind of brothers does Promise Keepers encourage us to become? When men first come together in a small group setting, Gorsuch and Schaffer tell us that above all everyone should be made to feel safe and comfortable:

> The first job of men's small groups is to learn complete acceptance: no judgment, no "I told you so" or "you should have known better." No hidden agendas! I'm not out to change you and you're not out to change me. . . . Complete acceptance, however, will create a safe place where men can really be themselves.[29]

The beginning of a men's group is a free-for-all with biblical discernment nowhere in sight. Suppose you attended the first meeting of a small group and a man were to confess that he killed someone in a drunk driving hit-and-run accident just hours before. Would you really do your best to make him feel "safe" so that he could really be himself?

"But that's such an extreme example," you protest.

Okay, suppose he simply confesses to having driven

while drunk on several occasions. Now what? Or suppose that he confesses that he is a drunkard. Or what about a man living in an adulterous relationship? What about a man who is thinking about leaving his wife for another woman? Didn't someone by the name of Paul once say that Christians were

> not to associate with any so-called brother if he should be an immoral person, or covetous, or an idolater, or a reviler, or a drunkard, or a swindler—not even to eat with such a one. . . Remove the wicked man from among yourselves (1 Cor. 5:11-13).

Calm down there, big fella. Don't you know about "complete acceptance?" Haven't you read Gorsuch and Schaffer? Don't you know about creating a "safe place" where men can really be their adulterous, covetous, reviling, drunken, and swindling selves?

Now we ask you, does Promise Keepers propose true Christian fellowship based on gospel truths, or is it simply secular small group theory parading in disguise?

One final aspect of the mentorship mandate is rather humorous: having been told that we need to mentor with someone older,[30] someone younger,[31] someone of kindred spirit,[32] someone of color,[33] not to mention being involved in a marriage support group,[34] where is there any time for the family? Ironically, the family gets lost in the process of supposedly learning how to be a better family man.

And that's always the problem with man-made solutions such as Promise 2. Like crooked arrows, they always end up missing their intended target.

---

[1] *SPPK*, p. 43.
[2] *Ibid.*, p. 45.

[3] Chip MacGregor, "Why Do I Need a Mentor?," *New Man*, January/February, 1995, vol. 2, no. 1, p. 71.

[4] *SPPK*, p. 59, emphasis added.

[5] *Ibid.*, p. 58, emphasis added.

[6] *Ibid.*, p. 55, emphasis added.

[7] *Ibid.*, p. 61, emphasis added.

[8] *New Man*, September/October, 1995, vol. 2, no. 5, p. 52.

[9] Gary Rosberg, "We're in This Together," *New Man*, November/December, 1995, vol. 2, no. 6, p. 63, emphasis added.

[10] *TPPK*, p. 4, emphasis added.

[11] *Brothers!*, p. 11, emphasis added.

[12] *SPPK*, p. 58.

[13] Kenneth Clatterbaugh, *M.E.N. Magazine*, "Whose Keepers, What Promises?," October 1995, emphasis added.

[14] *TPPK*, p. 123, emphasis added.

[15] *TPPK*, p. 129.

[16] *New Man*, November/December, 1994, vol. 1, no. 3, p. 39, emphasis added.

[17] Don Crossland, "The Trap of Addiction," January/February, 1995, vol. 2, no. 1, p. 54.

[18] *SPPK*, p. 96.

[19] *Ibid.*

[20] *Ibid.*

[21] Anon., *New Man*, March/April, 1995, vol. 2, no. 2, p. 12, emphasis added.

[22] "The Story of a Former Adulterer," *New Man*, July/August, 1995, vol. 2, no. 4, pp. 56-57.

[23] Ken Canfield, "Treat Him Like a Best Friend," *New Man*, November/December, 1995, vol. 2, no. 6, p. 54.

[24] *Brothers!*, p. 15.

[25] *Ibid.*

[26] *Ibid.*, p. 103.

[27] *Ibid.*

[28] *Ibid.*, p. 13.

[29] *Ibid.*, p. 14.

[30] *SPPK*, pp. 53-55.

[31] *Ibid.*

[32] *Ibid.*

[33] *Ibid.*, pp. 165-67, 170.

[34] *Ibid.*, pp.110-11.

ELEVEN

The Path to Purity—Promise 3

A Promise Keeper is committed to practicing spiritual, moral, ethical, and sexual purity.[1]

Some people are just cranky, and it seems they can find fault with anything. Perhaps some readers are wondering whether we are in this class, and what on earth we could possibly object to in this promise. Suppose the promise had simply said, "Be good!" Would we still object? Suppose it had been a vow not to kick the dog, would we still be sniffing out doctrinal problems?

Of course not. In *Seven Promises of a Promise Keeper*, the section devoted to this particular promise contains some admirable exhortation, and clear godly insights. For example, Tony Evans correctly identifies the heart of ethical compromise as the result of the American male losing a sense of his masculinity. He says, "I am convinced that the primary cause of this national crisis is the feminization of the American male."[2] He correctly points out that spiritual purity is the fountainhead of all purity.

Hard Teaching and Tender Hearts

Evans presents hard teaching the way men need to hear it.

Biblical love is commitment love. It has more to do with your actions than with your feelings. Any dog can satisfy his libido. It takes a really spiritually pure man to be faithful *regardless* of his passions . . .

If you've failed in the past, confess your sins to God. Then recommit yourself to your spiritual priorities. Get back on your feet, dust yourself off, and *"go and sin no more."*[3]

Hard teaching, biblically presented, results in tender hearts. Soft teaching, teaching that is soft on sin, results in hard hearts and hard people. In this respect, this emphasis on black and white ethical standards, with no slack anywhere, is long overdue. Along these lines, Gary Oliver says, "Now I know that in the process of becoming a godly man, there are no 'little' things."[4] Little compromises lead to great ones. In no small measure, Promise Keepers has had the positive impact which it has had because of this emphasis on integrity and purity, straight up. Men are tired of the defilement and guilt which comes from "small" sins. They want and need other men to draw a line, a line which echoes God's standards, and which consequently doesn't move from day to day.

The high standard is right and good. We live in a fallen world in which God works redemptively. This means that nothing can be *assumed* to be in submission to God. It can only be assumed to be in submission to Him, or *not* in submission to Him. Sin and disobedience are a tragic reality. Consequently, we must consider all things as a blessing, *or a curse*, depending upon its relationship to the Word of God. "An excellent wife is the crown of her husband, but she who causes shame is like rottenness in his bones" (Prov. 12:4). Women are a wonder to have around—or a horror.

When women are sexually disobedient, the dislocations in the lives of men can be severe. The Bible warns of the seductive woman: "This is the way of an adulterous woman: She eats and wipes her mouth, and says, 'I have done no wickedness'" (Prov. 30:20). The wisdom of God found in Proverbs brings with it as no small blessing the fact that it preserves a man from a horrible pit (2:16; 6:24; 7:5). This horrible pit is the mouth of an immoral woman; those who are hated by God will fall there (22:14). This must be seen by obedient faith, because an immoral woman looks good (7:10) and sounds good (5:3). Nothing is accomplished by Christians who deny the obvious. But the Bible teaches that when all is said and done, adultery is a form of suicide. "Whoever commits adultery with a woman lacks understanding; he who does so destroys his own soul" (6:32).

From the Heart

In the Sermon on the Mount, as Jesus teaches about integrity under the law of God, He also draws a hard line. As we have already seen, Christ teaches that obedience to the law is never a matter of external conformity; it is a question of heart loyalty. Put another way, the well-respected and "pious" tend to think about individual *sins*. The godly are constrained by the teaching of Christ to think about our condition of sinfulness, the fountainhead of all sins.

> You have heard that it was said to those of old, "You shall not commit adultery." But I say to you that whoever looks at a woman to lust for her has already committed adultery with her in his heart. If your right eye causes you to sin, pluck it out and cast it from you; for it is more profitable for you that one of your members perish, than for your whole body to be cast into hell. And if your right hand causes you to sin, cut it off and cast it from you; for it is more profitable for you that one of your members perish, than for your whole body to be cast into hell (Matt. 5:27-30).

Jesus applies the law of God in a way which "decent"

people do not like. His application makes all men adulterers; His teaching is plain and very blunt. We see this principle when Christ taught about money. "And He said to them, "You are those who justify yourselves before men, but God knows your hearts. For what is highly esteemed among men is an abomination in the sight of God" (Luke 16:15). What a fearful thought! God knows the heart. And what does He see there? "For out of the heart proceed evil thoughts, murders, adulteries, fornications, thefts, false witness, blasphemies" (Matt. 15:19; *cf.* Mark 7:21). The source of sins is sin. The source of these sins is the human heart. Christ's teaching goes right to the heart of the matter, and He cuts sin no slack.

Now the biblical standard of sexual morality is not difficult to understand. God requires absolute purity, mental and physical, prior to marriage, and absolute fidelity, mental and physical, after marriage. Just because this truth is easy to understand does not mean it is easy to do, but it nevertheless *is* easy to understand. This standard is clearly embodied in this commitment made by Promise Keepers. The clarity of this requirement means that those who want to get around it, while thinking to themselves that they are actually obeying it, or thinking that their disobedience isn't all that bad, must resort to various ingenuities. Peter tells us that we are to abstain from various fleshly lusts which war against our souls (1 Pet. 2:11). As with all warfare, sometimes the assault is straight up the middle, while other times subterfuge is employed. If a man is tempted to head down to a strip joint while the family thinks he is shopping for a Mother's Day present, we could consider that as an "assault up the middle." But there are many other snares which are not nearly so blatant, and which ensnare men just as effectively.

Head Games

Some men daydream at length about sexual activity with women other than their wives, and sanctify this in their minds by including marriage vows as part of the daydream. In other words, in their daydreams they are lawfully single again (perhaps a grieving widower? Such a trial, really . . .), and then because they marry their new partner, whatever goes on is okay, right? Not right. Wanting another man's wife as one's own wife is right at the heart of breaking the tenth commandment (Ex. 20:17).

Another contrivance is established by the amateur sociologist, who watches programming and reads magazines he ought not in the name of keeping a thoughtful finger on America's pulse. "This is an important film for understanding postmodern culture . . ." He is helped in this in the fact that half the people at church have seen this important film too. Important films are distinguished from dirty movies by three biblical criteria, but we forget what they are.

Then another man silently blames his wandering mind on his wife. "If she met my needs . . . If she only . . . And if she . . ." A man who thinks this way is like someone who wants to buy a new house because the lawn there is freshly mowed, and the lawn where he lives isn't. He may not be courageous enough to sin openly, but he justifies indulging his mental lust by saying that his wife would have no right to complain if she knew because she is the one who sets him up. The problem here is that lust is not just a sin against a wife; it is also a sin against God (Ps. 51:4). Moreover, a man who has an unresponsive wife is responsible to God for that too.

Someone else buys the pop-adage that "it doesn't matter where you get your appetite, as long as you eat at home." And so he tells himself that he is actually working hard to improve his relationship with his wife this way. To which we might answer, "Way to sacrifice, big guy." A variation of this involves mental scissors and library paste, and self-justifying editorial skills. One of us once had a conversation with a Christian man who said that whenever he was looking at another woman's naked body, he just imagined his wife's face on her. But the Bible doesn't tell us to be satisfied with our wives from the neck up (Prov. 5:19). Consequently, it should be no big surprise to find out that all such promised "improvements" in the marriage relationship are fleeting at best.

A man cannot contrive a defense for this out of the fact that his wife "doesn't mind" if he looks around. Again, sexual fidelity is not a duty a man owes primarily to his wife; it is a duty a man owes to God concerning his wife. Put another way, a wife has no authority to give this kind of permission. Only God may give it, and He has not done so.

Another man has discovered that there is nothing like sin to turn one into a precise exegete. "Jesus said not to lust after a woman. But what does *lust* refer to anyway? What's the Greek word? And what is the exact dividing line between appreciation of beauty on the one hand, and lust on the other? We have to be careful not to go beyond the Scriptures." The point is simultaneously well-taken and much-abused. The real issue is simple honesty. As we have already noted, the sin of lust is distinguished from temptation to lust (and appreciation of beauty), but this does not mean that the realm of temptation is a good place for a man to stand, however nice the view. One of the simpletons in the Book of Proverbs lost his very life for being stupid *before* he got into overt adultery. "With her enticing speech she caused him to yield, with her flattering lips she seduced him" (Prov. 7:21).

A popular head game with Christian men is the idea that "I can still do this, and still not fall." But when a man has gotten it into his head that the goal of his sanctification is to be as close to sin as he can get without actual sin, he has already joined the ranks of the simple and deserves everything he gets. The consistent biblical answer is that a response to such head games enables a man truly to rejoice (Prov. 5:18). And in their commitment to "practicing spiritual, moral, ethical, and sexual purity" Promise Keepers has stated the biblical standard well.

A Question of Integrity

Consequently, the first criticism we have of Promise Keepers at this point has nothing to do with the clear stand it has taken in this area. The promise to remain pure is an important commitment. Our problem is that this biblical stand is not taken across the board, or all the way down to the bottom. Because of the eclectic approach to teaching taken by Promise Keepers, genuine discrepancies—some of them moral and ethical—appear throughout Promise Keepers literature. Where there is error, it of course presents a discrepancy with Scripture. But it also presents a discrepancy with the sound standard which Promise Keepers raises elsewhere.

Some of its teachers do quite a fine job of taking a scriptural and ethical stand. But unfortunately, some do not. The result is inconsistency—the very thing which results in broken promises on an individual level. This inconsistency in teaching is just that—*inconsistency*. It is not consistency in poor teaching; it presents an odd mix of sound biblical insight, and modern psychological noodling.

For example, take a businessman on the road who is tempted with pornography. In *Seven Promises of a Promise Keeper*, the exhortation is clear and pointed— "Don't!" "God's call to virginity before marriage is unequivocal . . . For us married men, sexual purity means reflecting God's absolute faithfulness to us in our faithfulness to our wives. Adultery can take many forms."[5] This teaching is clear, pointed, and scriptural. But this standard is not consistently applied. None

of us would think much of a Christian man who was proud
of himself for reading porn, or consorting with prostitutes,
only on every other business trip. The trips without infidelity would not "balance" or "even out" his adulteries.

But in a very similar way, Promise Keepers is not uni-
formly hard on sin. If every other speaker, or every other
writer, is unfaithful to the scriptural standard, then the problem of the organization as a whole is infidelity. Tragically,
this is a very real problem. For example, contrast some of
the sound, biblical statements made above with the teaching
of one Promise Keeper spokesman, Robert Hicks, who
wanted to celebrate sins as rites of passage, as we discussed
earlier.

Needless to say, young men who have fallen into sin
should be taught that forgiveness is found in Christ. And of
course they should be treated with respect as they are rebuked. But a key portion of that respect is shown by treating them as young men who are *responsible* for what they
do.

So a marked difference both in content and tone stands
between Evans exhorting those who have sinned to confess
that sin, and to stop, and Hicks saying that those who have
fallen should be congratulated for merely being human.
Unfortunately, it is the compromise of the one which ad-
versely affects the integrity of the other. When a glove is
dropped in the mud, the mud doesn't get glovey. Occasional
infidelity is infidelity. Sporadic integrity is not integrity.
Listen to the prophet Haggai:

> . . . the word of the Lord came by Haggai the prophet,
> saying, "Thus says the Lord of hosts: 'Now, ask the priests
> concerning the law, saying, "If one carries holy meat in the
> fold of his garment, and with the edge he touches bread or
> stew, wine or oil, or any food, will it become holy?"'" Then
> the priests answered and said, "No." And Haggai said, "If
> one who is unclean because of a dead body touches any of
> these, will it be unclean?" So the priests answered and said,

"It shall be unclean." Then Haggai answered and said, "'So is this people, and so is this nation before Me,' says the Lord, 'and so is every work of their hands; and what they offer there is unclean'" (Hag. 2:10-14).

The principle is clear—if someone spills catsup on the front of a clean white shirt, we say the shirt is dirty. We do not say that it is still 97% clean. Some of the teaching on sexual and moral purity which comes from the Promise Keepers is quite good. But some of it is atrocious, and it is this latter teaching which unfortunately establishes the practical standard set by the Promise Keepers.

A Matter of the Heart

But we must go further than this. To continue our illustration, if a man were periodically unfaithful to his wife, but believed himself to be doing well because he was trying to avoid adultery on *some* of his trips, we would not be wrong to question his understanding of the biblical doctrine of sanctification. But throughout Scripture, a proper understanding of sanctification is directly connected to, and built upon, our understanding of justification. Moral and ethical purity cannot be divorced from a proper understanding of the gospel. In Scripture, the problems caused by moral law alone, apart from the doctrines of saving grace, were pronounced and obvious. Consider Paul's struggle with the moral law before his conversion. "I would not have known sin except through the law. For I would not have known covetousness unless the law had said, 'You shall not covet.'" (Rom. 7:7). Prior to regeneration and salvation, the law is a terror. For someone who does not understand justification by faith, as Saul the Pharisee did not, the law becomes a torment.

But once someone is converted, the law of God ceases to be a terror and condemnation to him. It becomes a delight

(Ps. 119:16), and a source of light to him. The godly man draws wisdom from Scripture, as water from a well. He no longer tries to use the law of God as a ladder to climb up to heaven. He now knows that only Christ can bring us to heaven. But the law is now a delightful source of information concerning what it is to live a godly life. And because we now love God through Christ, we crave that information. What the law could not do (make us right with God), God did through sending His Son to be a sin offering, in order that the righteous requirements of the law might be fully met in us (Rom. 8:4). Because we are free in Christ, we are not free *to* sin; we are free *from* sin. Being under grace, and not under law, means that sin no longer has dominion over us (Rom. 6:14).

Now Christ sets the standard clearly, but He does not just teach that real adultery is a matter of the heart. He also says that such inner adultery is of immense importance to the sinner. How important is it? Rather than fall under the judgment of God for sin, the sinner should prefer self-mutilation. If removing eyes and hands would remove sin, then sin is serious enough to do exactly that. Because the context of this passage is the teaching about adultery on one side and then divorce on the other, it is likely that Christ is alluding to the preferability of self-castration as opposed to undergoing the wrath of God.

But the problem is that self-mutilation will not work to restrain sin. Neither will asceticism, or a harsh treatment of the body (Col. 2:23). Neither will purity be achieved through the action of making a promise. What is the offending member? What brings me to sin? What produces sin in me? What must therefore be cut off? The answer is that my offending member is my *heart*. The doctrine is that I must have a new heart, or I will die.

We must therefore get the doctrines of justification and regeneration straight in our minds. A tremendous amount of mischief has resulted from confusion at this point. We are not born again because we made certain decisions. Rather, we have repented and believed because God has given us the new birth. If my old heart had been capable of repentance and belief, then I did not need a new heart. I would simply have needed to improve upon the old one.

What does God promise through His prophet? "I will give you a new heart and put a new spirit within you; I will take the heart of stone out of your flesh and give you a heart of flesh" (Ez. 36:26). Who will do this? The only One who can—the Lord God. And see the result in verse 27—"And I will put My Spirit within you and cause you to walk in My statutes, and you will keep My judgments and do them."

Jesus does call His followers to a genuine submission to the law of God—complete integrity in every area. If we cannot, then we must cry out for a new heart. If we are believers who have drifted into compromise, then we must confess our sin to Him. He is faithful and just to forgive. Our new hearts enable us to look to Him for all our righteousness. True purity is found only there; He is the only Promise Keeper.

Weeping with the Enemy?

But there has been a tragic blurring of the biblical doctrine of justification by faith alone. Now in the history of the church, the combination of strict and high moral standards and a muddy understanding of the free grace of the gospel has always resulted, in the long run, in various forms of legalism and hypocrisy. The problem is not the high moral standard—for that we are grateful. But we must recognize that in Scripture the only possible foundation for righteous living is the grace of God in Christ. But in order to build upon the foundation of grace, this grace must be preached, thoroughly explained, vigorously defended, carefully articulated, and zealously guarded against possible distortions and corruptions. Thus far, this has not been done by Promise Keepers—an organization works in concert with other organizations which are the avowed enemies of a biblically-defined grace.

Justifying grace does not introduce an opportunity to live at a lower level. It brings in the only possible way in which a sinner can live at a higher level. "For I say to you, that unless your righteousness exceeds the righteousness of the scribes and Pharisees, you will by no means enter the kingdom of heaven" (Matt. 5:20). Now our only possible standard of righteousness is that revealed in the law of God. But our condition is sinful and wretched; we all fall far short of the perfection required by the law. Our condition is at war with the holiness of God's law. The only thing which can reconcile us to that perfection is the imputation of the righteousness of Jesus Christ. If that imputation of righteousness—justification again—is not understood with an evangelical and saving faith, then the only possible alternative is some man-made attempt at "reconciliation."

The Great Divorce

But man-made "reconciliations" are always attempts to bring the law of God down to us, down to a "more realistic" level. This means that as Promise Keepers endeavors to "raise the standard" on its current foundation, the results will necessarily fail. This pattern is already clearly visible in the Promise Keepers literature. For just one example, in a Promise Keeper book on marriage, *Strategies for a Successful Marriage*, one of the co-authors described a divorce he went through in this way:

> I agreed . . . that his idea could make a worthwhile book, but not one I could write then or even now. At the time I was completely exhausted, psychologically and emotion-

ally, from paddling upstream; so I took the easier way out, drifted with the current and took the plunge of divorce. Not until a latter-day mentor, Glenn Wagner, came along—with his own designs for a book on succeeding in marriage—could I fulfill the promise I made eight years earlier to John Alexander. What you hold in your hands is that book.[7]

What we actually have in our hands is a book co-authored by a divorced man who certainly sees divorce as an unhappy event, and certainly unfortunate, but who never mentions the divorce in moral, covenantal terms—we see no mention of sin, compromise, moral failure, broken promises, *etc.* We are not saying that a divorced man cannot speak about his divorce in a way that is edifying to other men. But in order to be truly edifying, the language must reflect the standards of Scripture (sin, covenant-breaking, *etc.*), not the standards of the modern American business world (mistakes, failed missions, *etc.*). The standards are set by God, not by anyone else, not even our wives. And this leads us right into Promise 4.

---

[1] *SPPK*, pp. 8, 69.
[2] *Ibid.*, p. 73.
[3] *Ibid.*, pp. 80-81.
[4] *Ibid.*, p. 89.
[5] *Ibid.*, p. 94.
[6] *TMJ*, p. 188.
[7] *SSM* p. 8.

TWELVE

House on the Rock—Promise 4

A Promise Keeper is committed to building strong marriages and families through love, protection, and biblical values.[1]

Once we have been set free in our justification, we find that our freedom has other direct applications. Because we now live by every word that proceeds from the mouth of God (Deut. 8:3), we do not have to live according to man-made standards. The definition of what constitutes a good husband is set down permanently by God in Scripture. This means that a whole bunch of other entities do not get to decide what a good husband is, or what a good husband does. The standard for godly husbandry is not set by our culture at large, talk show hosts, psychobabble books, seminars, the church, or even our wives.

He Said, She Said

Any discussion of the appropriate standard for Christian husbands in marriage raises a very real concern with what may be called an emphasis of the Promise Keepers movement. Throughout *Strategies for a Successful Marriage*, an assumption is made that the feminine expectations for marriage are accurate, and that the masculine expectations are not. The man must learn to conform his behavior to the expectations of his wife. In the words of E. Glenn Wagner and Dietrich Gruen, "I should find out what my wife's expectations are and then commit myself to doing everything within my power to meet them. . . ."[2] But a Christian man should first ask, are the expectations of my wife biblical? Why should we try to accomplish something which God has not instructed us to accomplish? If we obey God with regard to our wives, then their *needs* will certainly be met. But this is not necessarily the same thing as meeting their *expectations*. A marriage exists in order to glorify God through evangelical obedience on the part of both husband and wife. Neither spouse is to submit to the other's standards for marriage; they both are to submit to Christ's.

When we consider the point here, we must remember that a woman's expectations may be unscriptural. For example, what is to be done with a quarrelsome woman? Proverbs has much to say about the clamor of foolish women (9:13). It is better to live in the corner of an attic than to be around a contentious woman (21:9; 25:24). It is better to be out in the desert than to be around a quarrelsome woman (21:19). To be in a house that leaks during a downpour is about the same (27:15). In short, the Bible teaches that mouthy and quarrelsome women are a pain in the neck. If a Christian man finds himself in this situation, he is responsible before God to love his wife as Christ loved the church, but this does not mean that he is to "find out what her expectations are." He already knows what this quarrelsome woman's expectations are—that is his problem.

The standards for the behavior of husbands and wives are set by the Bible. As we have seen, a foolish woman is a destructive force. In contrast, what are the characteristics of the obedient woman? Husbands are commanded to rejoice sexually with their wives (5:18); they are commanded to be enraptured (5:19). This is something the husband is commanded to do, and is able to do, but not alone. In other words, a godly wife can outdo all the one-night stands in the world. However, both his and her expectations in this area are set by Scripture.

The Bible teaches, "The wise woman builds her house, but the foolish pulls it down with her hands" (14:1). A husband needs to know quite a bit more than what his wife's expectations are—he must also know whether she is wise or foolish in her expectations. His marriage may be a great trial for him, but a good wife is a tangible sign of God's blessing (18:22). Put another way, a prudent wife is from the Lord (19:14). It is important to note that a recognition of a wife's sins in no way removes the responsibility a man has for the state of his marriage. It simply means that as the husband he is responsible to submit everything to the authority of Scripture.

But the shift in emphasis advocated by Promise Keepers is difficult for many Christian men to see. For example, throughout *Strategies for a Successful Marriage* many scriptural things are said about the manner in which husbands should treat their wives. Husbands are to treat their wives in a godly and gracious manner. Wagner and Gruen reaffirm this truth:

> We know that we're supposed to be kind, tender-hearted, gentle, patient, forgiving (Colossians 3:12-14). Such virtues are not feelings we conjure up or actions we do only when we feel like it. Husbands, "clothe yourselves" with these virtues, and as a coverall "put on love." Whether you want to or not, you get dressed every morning. For the same reason—whether we feel like it or not—we should wear this spiritual attire/attitude toward our wives. Such love not only covers (holds together) your virtues but also covers (forgives) a multitude of sins and irreconcilable differences (Proverbs 10:12, Romans 13:8-10, 1 Peter 4:8).[3]

This passage is on the money; it is a good description of how husbands should behave toward their wives. But it is not enough to do what we do in a biblical manner; we must also be doing biblical things. The standards for what we are to do are set by Scripture, not by the expectations of our wives.

Vocational Rehabilitation in the Home

God calls men to serve Him in their vocational callings. God in His wisdom teaches us that men cannot fulfill their ordained functions without help from their wives, and He therefore requires men to love and honor their wives. This emphasis and priority is important, as Paul teaches.

> For the man is not of the woman; but the woman of the man. Neither was the man created for the woman; but the woman for the man. . . . Nevertheless neither is the man without the woman, neither is the woman without the man, in the Lord. For as the woman is of the man, even so is the man also by the woman; but all things are of God (1 Cor. 11:8-9,11-12).

For Paul, the question of origins is important. The man was not created for the woman, but rather the other way around. A man's vocation and calling transcend that of meeting his wife's expectations. This should not make him haughty or distant—Paul also points out the mutual dependence that the sexes have. And as Paul insists elsewhere, men must love their wives as Christ loved the church (Eph. 5:25).

We must remember the lessons about men and women taught in Genesis, which is a book of beginnings. Here we see the beginning of the world, obviously, but also the beginning of marriage, and of the work to be done by husbands. Even our word vocation comes from the Latin *voco*, meaning "I call." A man's vocation is his calling under God.

> Then God blessed them, and God said to them, "Be fruitful and multiply; fill the earth and subdue it; have domin-

ion over the fish of the sea, over the birds of the air, and over every living thing that moves on the earth" (Gen. 1:28).

So God blessed Noah and his sons, and said to them: "Be fruitful and multiply, and fill the earth. And the fear of you and the dread of you shall be on every beast of the earth, on every bird of the air, on all that move on the earth, and on all the fish of the sea. They are given into your hand. Every moving thing that lives shall be food for you. I have given you all things, even as the green herbs" (Gen. 9:1-3).

These commands from God have historically been called the cultural mandate. Before the Fall, God expressly gave dominion to mankind over all creation. This is seen in the passage from the first chapter of Genesis. But God reiterates this charge to Noah. Noah lived after the Fall, and this mandate is given immediately after a stupendous judgment on sin. The presence of sin obviously does not lift or remove the cultural mandate.

Moreover, the language of the mandate assumes that generations downstream will continue to operate in terms of the mandate. We must carefully consider the words of Psalm 8. Contrary to the modern assumption of groups like *Earth First*, man is not an intruder on this planet. We are stewards; the earth was entrusted to us. The author of the book of Hebrews takes this passage from the Psalms and applies it to mankind in Christ. Consider his application of the psalm. The mandate remains in force for impotent man, but that impotence is removed in Christ.

For He has not put the world to come, of which we speak, in subjection to angels. But one testified in a certain place, saying: What is man that You are mindful of him, or the son of man that You take care of him? You have made him a little lower than the angels; You have crowned him with glory and honor, and set him over the works of Your hands. You have put all things in subjection under his feet. For in that He put all in subjection under him, He left nothing that is not put under him. But now we do not yet see all things put under him. But we see Jesus, who was made a little lower than the angels, for the suffering of death crowned with glory and honor, that He, by the grace of God, might taste death for everyone. For it was fitting for Him, for whom are all things and by whom are all things, in bringing many sons to glory, to make the captain of their salvation perfect through sufferings (Heb. 2:5-10).

Christian men are part of this mandate. God's call to the believing man includes his vocation in a central way as we will see in more detail in chapter 15. What a man does is not just a detached "job" (Eph. 2:8-10). While a man must honor, love, and cherish the one given to him to help him in his ordained task, he must not begin to think that he was created for her. He was created to do something else under God, and she was created as ideally suited to help him do it. The cultural mandate is to masculine vocation. Wives, of course, are essential to this process—we cannot accomplish anything worthwhile without their help, and we cannot have their help if we refuse to treat them right. But it is help which they offer.

Is There a Man in the House?

Essential to the fulfillment of a masculine vocation is masculinity. It is here that the modern evangelical church falls far short. Far from answering the sin of the world at this point, we are often ahead of the world in the sin of effeminacy. Men are called to serve and love God in all that they do, and to do so as men.

The contrast between this vision and the vision of the godly husband in the Promise Keepers literature is stark. "The ultimate goal Susan and I have for our marriage is to be more in love with each other at the end of our days than on the day we got married . . ."[4] Wagner and Gruen argue that families should draft mission statements. One of the benefits of this is that family "mission statements allow for power-sharing that prohibits anyone from making unilateral or random decisions contrary to your stated mission and goals."[5]

They also say, "The macho idea that men must make all the decisions, or have the final say, is not what marriage is about. Marriage is about a vibrant partnership, two coming together as one—and those two submerging their wills and living for the glory of God."[6]

Because the wife's expectations for a husband are treated as normative in Promise Keepers literature, it is not surprising that "recovering the romance" is a very important goal for the Promise Keepers.

> Put yourself in the all-too-familiar scenario of the husband-and-wife couple who are your friends, but have lost the romantic spark in their marriage. The husband comes to you seeking counsel about what to do to bring romance back and save his loveless marriage. He is eager to do whatever it takes to score husbanding points. What would you say to him?[7]

A good marriage is here defined as one which has that romantic spark, and a bad marriage is one in which the romance is missing. This is not the biblical emphasis. "Romance" is comparable to the curtains and carpet in a home. They help to make for pleasant surroundings, and in their place they are important. But they are no substitute for the concrete work necessary at the home's foundation—the concrete of covenant commitment.

But harmony in the home deepends upon a biblical masculinity, which provides the strength of that covenant commitment. At the center of each home should be a dependable man, a godly husband to the wife, and an immovable rock of a father for the children. He establishes and maintains his dominion through service, and not through domineering (Mark 9:35). In the home, one of the most important ways a man can sacrifice his own interests is through providing the leadership which the family needs from him. In this context, a servant's heart does not drift about, saying, "Gosh, I don't know. What do *you* want me to do?"

Men, of course, should be kind and pleasant to their wives and children, and the Scripture sternly forbids harshness in the home (Col. 3:19-21). But being "nice" does not exhaust the duties placed upon a man by the Lord. Many nice men, through lack of leadership, have driven their wives and children to the point of exasperation.

As mentioned earlier, soft leadership produces hard people. Hard leadership, provided it is biblically hard, results in tender people. Soft leadership never rebukes, never disciplines, and the results for the home are often gross. David was an indulgent father, and his son Amnon raped his half-sister. His son Absalom killed Amnon and later rebelled against his father. A soft father sired hard sons. Eli was another indulgent father and had sons who would sleep with the women who gathered at the tabernacle of the Lord. Soft leadership led to the harshness of rape, murder, and incest. In the modern world, we may add the fruit of drug abuse, divorce, sodomy, insolence, immorality, suicide, and all the rest.

Men must lead and protect their wives. When men neglect their wives, the world often sees the results of the husband's sin in the wife. When the results of this neglect show up in an obvious way through the wife's infidelity, drunkenness, obesity, *etc.*, everyone shakes his head and wonders what got into her. But the hardness of sin in her was brought into the world through the softness of his abdication. Men must be masculine for their wives and children; they must be hard *for* their wives, not hard *on* them.

Contra Mundum

But at the same time, our culture is at war with masculinity. This means that the men who are equipped to maintain peace in their homes will be men at war beyond the front door. A man who has what it takes to provide peace, stability, and security in his home will be just the kind of man who is embattled outside. Our world system is hostile to the kind of masculinity which is capable of guiding and protecting the godly home. Centuries ago, in the great battle over the Trinity, Athanasius was told at one time that the whole world was against him. Then let it be known, he said, that Athanasius is *contra mundum*—against the whole world. In the same way, the biblical man should know that his scriptural hardness, the necessary protective fence for his family, will always provoke a hostile response whenever he is out in the world.

When this kind of response is the result of faithfulness to the truth, and not the result of being obnoxious, we should rejoice when it happens. Jesus taught us that if everyone thinks we are wonderful, then we are doing something seriously wrong (Lk 6:26). Unfortunately, the false identification of truth and haughtiness can be found in the church as well. Because our culture at large considers the emasculation of men to be the norm, effeminate expectations for men have inundated the church.

So confusion reigns. Because there is a dearth of godly examples, some within the church have resorted to chest-pounding substitutes for biblical masculinity. Instead of a biblically confident leadership, we see arrogance, pride, overweening conceit, self-centered financial habits, boasting, and so forth. This sort of counterfeiting is from men who are not mature in their masculinity; they are blowhards. We presume it is this kind of masculinity which Wagner and Gruen have in mind when they reject the "macho" leadership which has to have the final say. This kind of posturing is a problem, but contrary to Wagner and Gruen, it is not a problem caused by men functioning in their marriages as heads (Eph. 5:23).

True masculinity is easy to caricature. A Christian man who is living out a biblical masculinity may be slanderously accused of being proud, arrogant, too logical, self-willed, *etc.* In a very real way (and this is a central part of the tragedy of our modern church), we are put off by masculinity. We insist upon being led by women, or, if that cannot be done, by men who are endeavoring to become like women. Isaiah spoke of the problem this way. "As for My people, children are their oppressors, and women rule over them. O My people! Those who lead you cause you to err, and destroy the way of your paths" (Is. 3:12). A mark of how thoroughly we have been propagandized can be seen in how we react to such passages. Instead of seeing such biblical language as a slap at effeminate men, we think it is an insult to women.

It is ironic that this emphasis on keeping or recovering the romance in marriage, undercuts the promise being made here, which is to build "strong marriages and families through love, protection, and biblical values."

Romancing the Home?

Success and failure in any endeavor is always measured and determined by what the objective is believed to be. If a failed marriage is one in which the romance has departed, what happens when the parties believe the spark cannot be recovered? The marriage has already "failed." In the words of Wagner and Gruen, ". . . divorce *per se* is not the bogeyman. Divorce doesn't kill a marriage any more than a funeral director kills the corpse."[8]

But if this is the case, then a couple could be tempted to disobey Christ, and end their marriage, because the marriage has "already ended." It has already ended because it failed to meet the standards of a "successful" marriage. How's that for a circular argument? But viewed biblically, an unsuccessful marriage remains a marriage, and the covenant obligations remain fully in force. Nowhere in Scripture is a marriage defined in terms of "romance" or the domestic happiness of the partners. Indeed, it would have been difficult for the biblical writers to appeal to this defining concept of romantic love because it would not be invented until the eleventh century. As classical scholar C. S. Lewis observed:

> It seems—or it seemed to us till lately—a natural thing that love (under certain conditions) should be regarded as a noble or ennobling passion: it is only if we imagine ourselves trying to explain this doctrine to Aristotle, Virgil, St. Paul, or the author of Beowulf, that we become aware how far from natural it is . . .[9]

When a man falls out of love with his wife, or has behaved in such a manner that she has fallen out of love with him, their respective duties are completely untouched. Whether his emotions approve or not, he must give himself to her as Christ loved the church. Whether her emotions want to go along, she must respect and honor him. When these duties are faithfully performed, they create a climate in which our "pleasant" emotions may thrive. But whether they thrive or not, it is important to note that a successful marriage in biblical terms is one in which the vows made are biblical, and they are kept. There is no biblical imperative to include our emotional happiness as a defining standard. Again, Lewis:

> And, of course, the promise, made when I am in love and because I am in love, to be true to the beloved as long as I live, commits one to being true even if I cease to be in love. A promise must be about things that I can do, about actions: no one can promise to go on feeling in a certain way. He might as well promise never to have a headache or always to feel hungry.[10]

To reverse the order of actions and feelings is an attempt
to heap up the curtains and carpet for a foundation, and
build a house on top of the pile. When the inevitable crash
comes, and the partners go off to someone new who does
give them the feelings which they believe define a successful
union, they are committing adultery. They have fallen into
impurity because they sought to defend their marital purity
through a protective fence of emotional attachment. But
rather, we should seek to protect all that God has entrusted
to us through covenantal faithfulness, whether we feel like
it or not.

In this respect, Promise Keepers is simply reflecting the
broad acceptance by modern evangelicals of "romance-as-
foundation-for-marriage." But in order to call men back to
their covenant obligations, a different emphasis entirely is
needed.

A God to You and Your Seed

Throughout a book such as this, it is necessary to acknowledge clearly those things taught and passed on by
Promise Keepers which are truly valuable—and which are
necessary for many men today to hear and heed. For
an outstanding example, James Dobson's chapter in *Seven
Promises of a Promise Keeper* concerning a man and his family
correctly points out the importance of parental responsibility
in discipline. He says,

> According to the Christian values which govern my life,
> my most important reason for living is to get the baton—
> the gospel—safely in the hands of my children. Of course,
> I want to place it in as many other hands as possible, and
> I'm deeply devoted to the ministry to families that God
> has given me. *Nevertheless, my number one responsibility is
> to evangelize my own children.*[11]

Dobson clearly indicates that he does not believe that the salvation of our children is simply a matter of chance. He shows that winning our children is through the parents' "deep travail of prayer and faith." He points out, correctly, that

> If you doubt the validity of this assertion, may I suggest that you read the story of Eli in 1 Samuel 2-4. Here is the account of a priest and servant of God who failed to discipline his children. He was apparently too busy with the "work of the church" to be a leader in his own home. The two boys grew up to be evil young men on whom God's judgment fell.
>
> It concerned me to realize that Eli's service to the Lord was insufficient to compensate for his failure at home. Then I read farther in the narrative and received confirmation of the principle. *Samuel*, the saintly man of God, who stood like a tower of spiritual strength throughout his life, grew up in Eli's home. He watched Eli systematically losing his children, yet Samuel proceeded to fail with his family, too! That was a deeply disturbing truth. If God would not honor Samuel's dedication by guaranteeing the salvation of his children, will He do more for me if I'm too busy to do my "homework"?[12]

In a world of blame-shifting and evasion, Dobson's words are a fresh breeze. Men should spend biblical time with their families because doing so makes a difference. Although Dobson does not use the vocabulary of covenant and generational succession, as we would, his commitment to assuming responsibility for discipline and its results is clear and admirable. Eli did not effectively discipline his sons, and neither did Samuel. They are held up in Scripture as poor examples at this point, and Dobson passes this valuable lesson on to his readers.

Withhold Not Correction

However, when Promise Keepers gives something with the right hand, it should not take it away with the left. In the chapter just prior to Dobson's, Gary Smalley presented some principles for family living that are genuinely problematic. They are problematic because they are profoundly unbiblical.

Smalley was seeking to outline certain principles for resolving a typical family conflict. For purposes of illustration, he told the story of some friends, the Brawners, who had a son named Jason who was away at college. The potential conflict concerned Jason coming home with an earring. "None of the men in his family had ever worn an earring, and it just wasn't done among their circle of friends. Jason felt the roof might come off when Mom and Dad saw him."[13]

But Dad, according to Smalley, did just great.

> Finally, Dad saw it. "Hey-y-y, what's this?" he said.
> Jason thought, *Oh, no! He's going to rip it off my ear.*
> Suzette gently suggested, "Now, don't overreact."
> But Jim didn't react at all. Calmly and sensitively, he asked, "What's going on?"
> Jason answered, "Dad, everybody on the swim team has an earring. I knew you'd be upset, but Dad, I was the only guy who didn't have one. The seniors said either I do it or, you know, I'm in trouble."
> "If you want to wear the earring, that's your business," Jim answered. "It's not up to me. Only God knows how much I love you. Personally, I wouldn't wear an earring, but hey, I understand the pressure you were getting."[14]

Smalley goes on to say, "What the Brawners did is what I wish millions of families would do."[15] Unfortunately, his wish has been granted—millions of families are doing exactly this sort of thing. But it is not an example of harmony and understanding, but rather of abdication.

Now in analyzing this situation, a few disclaimers are necessary. It is not our purpose to address the actual situation as it happened with the Brawners, but rather with the situation as it was presented in the book for purposes of imitation. We were not there when it happened, but we have read the story as it was told, and have understood the lesson which Smalley wished the readers would draw from it. Neither is it our purpose to talk about earrings. The issue does not really concern the "grist" of the family conflict—it could have been over anything. Our central concern rather is how the conflict was handled.

The scenario laid out by Gary Smalley is an outstanding example of parental abdication. Consider the situation: a nineteen-year-old son came home from college having done something which he believed would make his parents angry. He nevertheless was willing to do this because of peer pressure at school. In other words, the opinion of the seniors on the swim team meant more to him than the opinion of his parents. Again, the issue is not the earring; the issue is the disrespect and contempt shown for his parents. In response to this, the young man's father said that he fully understood the pressure his son was getting.

Of course, we agree with Smalley that the father did well in not losing his temper over the earring. But at the same time, the father grievously failed when he refused to address a profound problem his son clearly had—an inability to resist ungodly pressure, even when the price of capitulation is hurting your family. Smalley said that by this abdication, this taking the easy way out, the Brawners "honored their son."[16] On the contrary, they returned his disrespect for them to him, along with some increase. They failed at just the point which Dobson addresses just a few pages later.

In discipline issues, many assume that the only choice presented to parents is between calm and "sensitive" abdication on the one hand, and "blowing your stack" on the other. But this is a false dilemma—why is it impossible for the father to take this time to teach his son a valuable lesson on the importance of doing things for the right reason?

Smalley has done the same thing Wagner and Gruen have done. Just as Wagner and Gruen suggest that husbands should let their wives set the pace in the home for their husbands, so Smalley has suggested letting children set the pace in the home for their parents. While parents should not exasperate their children (Eph. 6:4; Col. 3:21), they nevertheless are called to glorify God, not to meet the expectations of their children.

Sadly, Smalley is not alone. Another Promise Keepers author, Greg Johnson, wrote an entire article on how to be a "cool" dad—cool, of course, in the eyes of his children.[17] Like Smalley, Johnson holds up to us an example of a father who, though he kept his cool when his child inexplicably "earned" a "D" for goofing off too much in class, abdicated his headship in the home. As opposed to taking the lead in confronting his son, this father let his child do all the talking; he even allowed his child to suggest his own "punishment"—"two weeks without watching sports on TV."[18] O, the wages of sin! Again, the point is not the "D" grade or the specific "discipline" meted out. The point is that this father is touted as an example for us to follow when the only thing he is an example of is ungodly abdication. According to Johnson, "The issue was settled and [the father] didn't have to moralize once."[19] Way to go dad.

And being "cool" means we should rarely, if ever, use negatives with our children, or as *New Man* puts it, "Don't say don't." According to *New Man*, parents should "make a dedicated effort to remove as many [don'ts] as possible from [their] daily conversations with [their] children."[20] Instead of saying "Don't hit your sister," for instance, we are told instead, we should say "Play nicely with your sister," or "Be nice," or "Let's keep our hands to ourself."[21] But doesn't God repeatedly use "don'ts" with us as His children? Didn't He as our Heavenly Father command us as His children eight out of ten times saying "Thou shalt have no . . ." or "Thou shalt not . . ."? Aren't we supposed to model our parenting and discipline here on earth after how our Heavenly Father parents and disciplines us (Heb. 12:4-11)? Upon what biblical basis, then, does *New Man* urge us to purge negatives from our vocabularies in the home? Perhaps *New Man* should follow it's own advice—"Don't Say Don't!"

Not content to tell us, "Don't Say Don't," still another New Man article tells parents that when they must take an "unpopular" stand with their children, "Don't quote Scripture to them."[22] Admittedly, Scripture may not be a crowd pleaser if our only concern is how well we will do in the polls. But God has not called us as parents to be "popular." He has called us to be biblical. And to be biblical, we must constantly impart biblical truth to our children. While we should always watch our attitude as we do so, we are still commanded to create a climate in which Scripture thrives in the home:

> And these words which I am commanding you today, shall be on your heart; and you shall teach them diligently to your sons and shall talk of them when you sit in your house and when you walk by the way and when you lie down and when you rise up (Deut. 6:6-7).

Indeed, heaven and earth—and unbiblical advice on parenting—will pass away, but the Word of the Lord endures forever!

Of course, if parents have not laid the foundation for discipline when the children are young by, among other things, saying "don't" where necessary or quoting biblical truth where necessary, it will be difficult (if not impossible) to establish this authority when the children are grown. Too many parents indulge sin in their children when the children are small (and sin is "cute"), but when the child is grown, and can buy drugs, or wreck a car, or get pregnant, the parents try to establish standards for the home for the first time. Yet the standards should have been established long before. As Tony Evans has written, "if Dad doesn't provide spiritually responsible leadership in the home, baby is in big trouble."[23]

By contrast, the scenarios presented by Smalley and Johnson tragically illustrate that we in the evangelical church are far beyond help (but fortunately, not beyond grace). In other words, in a book promoted by a self-proclaimed masculine renewal movement, abdicating fathers are set before us as examples to imitate. It would be bad enough for us to be confronted with a teenage son who acted like Jason Brawner, and we did not know what to do about it. But our situation is far, far worse. We are given an answer, but the answer we are given is a summary and sample of our sin.

We still are heading in the wrong direction, and on the subject of family restoration, Promise Keepers, sadly, is a major part of the problem.

---

[1] *SPPK*, pp. 8, 101.

[2] *SSM*, p. 14.

[3] *Ibid.*, p. 16.

[4] *Ibid.*, p. 25, emphasis added.

[5] *Ibid.*, p. 27.

[6] *Ibid.*, p. 59, emphasis added.

[7] *Ibid.*, p. 88, emphasis added.

[8] *SSM*, p. 6.

[9] C.S. Lewis, *The Allegory of Love* (Oxford, England: Oxford University Press, 1936), p. 3.

[10] C.S. Lewis, *Mere Christianity* (New York, NY: Macmillan, 1943), p. 83.

[11] *SPPK*, p. 124, emphasis his.

[12] *Ibid.*, p. 123.

[13] *Ibid.*, p. 106.

[14] *Ibid.*

[15] *Ibid.*, p. 107.

[16] *Ibid.*, p. 108.

[17] "How to Be a 'Cool Dad'," *New Man*, November/December, 1995, vol. 2, no. 6, pp. 32-35.

[18] *Ibid.*, p. 34

[19] *Ibid.*

[20] Anon., "Don't Say Don't," *New Man*, March/April, 1996, vol. 3, no. 2, p. 15.

[21] *Ibid.*

[22] Tim Kimmel, "Dad's Dress Address," *New Man*, March/April, 1996, vol. 3, no. 2, p. 62.

[23] *SPPK*, p. 75.

❀ THIRTEEN ❀

For Members Only—Promise 5

A Promise Keeper is committed to supporting the mission of his church by honoring and praying for his pastor, and by actively giving his time and resources.[1]

We may chuckle at the antics of the once-famous "church lady" of Saturday Night Live fame. But few of us would be humored to learn that popular American culture has rightly perceived the church and the church lady to be nearly indistinguishable. What is so tragic is not the false caricature of the prude portrayed in the skit, but the far more serious fact that the church is seen to be led by women, albeit women who mean well.

Men as men have abdicated their covenantal responsibilities not only in their individual lives, and not only at home, but also in the church. In the words of Promise Keepers writer, Tony Evans, they have become a bunch of sissies.

Just as the Promise Keepers movement is to be commended for calling men sissies to their face and challenging them to exercise covenantal masculinity in their lives and homes, it also has commendably challenged men to exercise the same covenantal masculinity in the church. It has admirably supported the local church from the beginning. "From its inception," writes Dale Schlafer, Vice President of Church Relations for Promise Keepers,

Promise Keepers' commitment to the local church is perhaps *the* overriding principle driving the organization . . .
I want to reaffirm that commitment: *We are committed to the local church and the pastor of the local church!*[2]

And if that is all Promise 5 amounted to, our hearts
would leap for joy. Unfortunately, again, many Promise
Keepers speakers and writers take back with one hand what
they give with the other. Our concerns are not directed at
the intentions. We agree with Schlafer that the outreach of
Promise Keepers is not "meant to undermine the ministry
of a denomination already ministering to men. It is meant
to complement what the church is already doing."[3] Intentions are one thing, and reality quite another. Although
Promise Keepers may intend to strengthen the local church,
some of what it has taught may subtly undermine the local
church in very serious ways.

The Movement Mentality

The first way the Promise Keepers movement subtly
undermines the church is that it rivals the church as an institution. The movement itself is seen as the focal point of the
Holy Spirit's activity today as opposed to the church. Though
the Bible teaches us that the Holy Spirit calls people out
from the world to the church and causes them to grow in
grace through the proclamation of the Word and the administration of the ordinances of baptism and the Lord's supper, the Promise Keepers movement emphasizes the work
of God in individuals *as individuals.* At times it comes peril-
ously close to implying that the proclamation of the Word
and the administration of the ordinances are man-made obstructions to the free flow of God's grace to the individual at
stadium-styled pep rallies.

Promise Keepers minimizes the ordinances, when it
bothers to mention them at all. To its credit, Promise Keep-

ers has not baptized converts at its conferences or administered the Lord's supper *en masse*. This stand may be a reflection of a low view of the ordinances or it may be more of an
attempt not to fracture its fragile ecumenical coalition by
taking a public stand on the thorny issues surrounding the
ordinances: *e.g.*, should baptism be by sprinkling or immer-
sion? Should infants be baptized? Should Promise Keepers
lean toward transubstantiation, consubstantiation, the real
presence, or memorialism? Nevertheless, the movement is
still to be lauded for not usurping the celebration of the ordinances which belongs to the local church.

But in the absence of these ordinances, the movement
has predictably gravitated to its own rituals that have come
to take on the aura and importance of the ordinances—ceremonies featured at each conference to signify and seal the
benefits of the conference to its participants. Just think of
the now-famous "closing night coronation" or "blessing of
pastors" which raises the emotional pitch on the final evening
of the typical conference. During this event, pastors stream
to the front of the stadium while laymen rise to their feet to
give them a rousing, stadium-styled standing ovation, complete with cheers such as, "We love you!"

Certainly, pastors are to be loved and encouraged. But
when pastors come to see this "blessing" as "more important than [their] ordination,"[4] as one pastor recently put it,
something is out of whack. It is even more out of whack
when Promise Keepers uses such comments as public relations ploys to convince other pastors to attend its conferences. The praise of man more important than the divine
commission from God? Hardly.

To what can we attribute the movement mentality
spawned by Promise Keepers? Michael Horton has commented that there are two different approaches to religion,
the "sect mentality" and the "church mentality."

The whole history of revivalism is the history of one sweeping emotional sect movement after another. After the hype wears out, people go back to doing what they were doing before and very often, cynical about the whole thing. D. L. Moody's program of "muscular Christianity" and Billy Sunday's gospel of manhood were precursors of Promise Keepers. The revivals may have moved from tents to football stadiums, but the idea is basically the same. While Promise Keepers encourages the support of pastors, it actually bears the marks of the sect mentality in that the movement rather than the church is seen as the focal point of the Spirit's activity today. Historical Christianity teaches that the Spirit works through Word and sacrament, and these are offered by the church. But revivalism tends to suggest that the Spirit works directly with the individual heart and doesn't need these so-called man-made obstructions.[5]

Notice what Horton is saying. We may adopt the sect/movement mentality on the one hand or the church mentality on the other. We can go from one movement to another to try to satisfy what God has designed the church to satisfy in our Christian lives. We can stress the spontaneity of a movement or the stability of the church. Why not both? Because they are rival faiths, with rival ends and rival means. By opting for the movement mentality in any shape or form, we end up undermining the church.

The movement mentality fostered by Promise Keepers has a creeping effect in the life of the local church. Consider as but one example the account of what happened at one church the Sunday after a Promise Keepers conference. Prior to the sermon one pastor asked the men in his church to share their Promise Keepers testimonies. And share they did.

Man after man got up, sharing stories and telling what he had gained from the experience. There were tears and laughter and resolutions to be different from now on. It became clear that the men's testimonies would have to serve as a sermon that Sunday.[6]

While hearing testimonies of the work of Christ in the lives of His people is encouraging to the body, not even testimonies can compare with the power of the Word of God as proclaimed by one of God's ordained servants in faithfulness to His Word. In fact, the Bible teaches us that the Word proclaimed by an ordained teacher is the primary means God has given to lead unbelievers to Christ and to sanctify God's people (Rom. 10:17; Jn. 17:17; 2 Tim. 4:2). It causes us to grow in the grace and knowledge of our Lord and Savior Jesus Christ. It should not be replaced with testimonials, no matter how well-intentioned.

The Groupy Mentality

Just as disturbing as the movement mentality and related to it is what we call the groupy mentality—the promotion of small groups outside the ministry of the local church. Even if the small groups spawned by Promise Keepers are intended to supplement the ministry of the local church, in practice, they usually end up supplanting it.

Promise Keepers authors and speakers wrest passages from their context to justify the formation of small groups. They take texts describing the church as a whole and apply them to small groups. For example, we are asked "Will we insist on going it alone or will we become part of a group of men and assume our role as a brother in Christ?"[7] Nowhere does the New Testament talk about a small group study apart from the oversight of the local church. When the New Testament talks about the brethren, it is talking about men and women in particular or regional churches.

While it is undoubtedly true that "Christ never wanted His disciples to live out their Christian lives alone,"[8] the small group is not the primary place for men to get connected. That is the role of the church. While there is certainly nothing wrong with small group studies under the oversight of the local church, such studies ought not to become a substitute for fellowship and worship in the local church. Yet, by uncritically applying verses speaking of the church to small groups (*e.g.*, Acts 2:42, Heb. 10:24-25, Matt. 18:15-17), Promise Keepers blurs the distinction between the two and subtly undermines the role of the church in the process.

Sometimes Promise Keepers authors come right out and exalt the group over the church by mandating that men join a small group, without ever mentioning the local church. A Promise Keepers study guide, *Daily Disciplines for the Christian*, for instance, never even mentions the role of the church in the life of the believer. In another publication, Howard G. Hendricks and son William recently wrote:

> If you are new to the faith or a fairly young believer, we strongly urge you to seek out a small group of men who together can serve as your mentors. *It could make a vital, live-or-die difference in your spiritual journey!*

Sure, Hendricks and son improve upon *Daily Disciplines* by mentioning the church later in their article, but only as one place among many for men to look for men to join a small group. And what should be the guiding concern when finding men to join your small group? That they be Promise Keepers: "(f)ind out who else is a Promise Keeper and invite them to join you on a regular basis."[10] While we are not saying that we cannot have fellowship with those outside the local church, we are saying that it is wrong for Promise Keepers to view the local church as simply a means to the end of the small group. This is to stand Scripture on its head.

The main problem with the groupy mentality is that the Bible already has a word for mentor: *elder*. Or, if you prefer, *pastor*. By encouraging men to find men, whether inside or outside the local church, to fuel their small groups, Promise Keepers actually undermines the role of the elders and the role of the local church in discipling men and helping them grow in grace. Promise Keepers actually undermines the local church itself by promoting groups which exist outside the local church and apart from its oversight. Never are men told in Promise Keepers literature to set up a small group under the oversight of the local church.

What ends up happening is that the small groups fostered by the Promise Keepers end up functioning like pseudo-churches. The groups have pseudo-leaders, regardless of whether they have been ordained or have fulfilled the qualifications set forth in the New Testament (1 Tim. 3:1-7; Titus 1:5-9). The groups have pseudo-teaching from books and study guides replete with inaccuracies. The groups even have pseudo-discipline. What the groups don't have, however, is the oversight of elders, the public proclamation of the Word from those ordained and properly trained to teach it, the administration of the ordinances, and the exercise of admonition and discipline. And they can't have them because they were entrusted by Christ to the church alone.

Christ, the Original Small Group Leader?

The only thing even remotely resembling biblical proof of the need for men to join a small group study outside the local church is the example of Christ, who, according to Geoff Gorsuch and Dan Shaffer, "chose to live out His life and ministry in the context of a small group of men. If He felt He needed brothers, how much more do we?"[11]

But did the sinless Christ, the second member of the eternal Godhead, really need anything in this respect—a small group of men with whom to have fellowship? As the One through whom all things were made, Christ did not need fellowship with the disciples in order to fulfill His divine calling. To suggest that He had any such need is to denigrate the fact that He was and is, in the words of the Nicene creed, "very God of very God." He had no "need" for fellowship with the disciples if for no other reason than that, as a member of the triune Godhead, He enjoyed perfect union and communion—perfect unity and fellowship—with the Father and the Spirit from all eternity (Gen. 1:26; Jn. 17:5, 11, 21-23).

What's more, Christ's fellowship with the disciples does not represent a paradigm for small group fellowship apart from, or even alongside, the church, as Gorsuch and Shaffer would have it. Christ's fellowship with the disciples was nothing less than the Head of the church with part of His body (Eph. 1:22-23), or, to use another Pauline metaphor, the cornerstone along with the foundation (2:20). If the example of Christ proves anything, it proves that we, like the disciples, need to become part of a local body under the headship of Christ and His appointed overseers in that local body. But let us never forget that *it is our need, not Christ's* that constrains us to join the church. Christ doesn't need us. We need Him. And while small groups may, under certain circumstances, supplement our involvement in the church, they should never supplant that involvement or the accountability that flows from it.

Our Little Secret

Not only does the Promise Keepers movement spawn small groups which function like, and hence, compete with, the local church, it also fosters unbiblical practices within those groups that positively undermine the ministry of the local church. As just one example, Gorsuch and Shaffer tell us that for men in a small group to move beyond being mere acquaintances to being true friends, they need to promise to keep all information shared in the group strictly confidential:

> For men to feel safe and move on to second base [become friends as opposed to mere acquaintances], they need to

know that the things they share will not go beyond the group. Trust is difficult to build, but it is even harder to rebuild. Trust is a precious commodity to be protected at all costs. Once trust is gone from a group, there is little chance of moving on in the quest for Christlikeness. So agree to a *covenant of confidentiality*. Without it, other covenants cannot follow.[12]

Later, these same authors explain in more detail what the covenant of confidentiality entails. Men are supposed to covenant as follows:

> What goes on in this group stays here. I will say nothing that may be traced to my covenant partners [the other men in the group].[13]

Now every believer, at one point or another, has known a foghorn—the "deeply concerned" Christian who just can't resist the urge to tell everyone what others are struggling with, even piously dressed up as a prayer request—"We should all remember Jack in prayer, that he would have the strength to overcome his temptation to steal from the cash register at work." And certainly such Christians need to learn a lesson or two about confidentiality.

While we all need to learn to build trust by keeping certain facts confidential that do not need to be broadcast on the evening news, no Christian can enter into a "covenant of confidentiality" without putting himself into a situation where he may have to disobey Christ and imperil the church in the process. Some things are to remain between brothers, but others, depending upon the circumstances, must be brought to the church. A covenant of confidentiality, however, would prevent Christians from doing so. It would also prevent the church from dealing with the situation since it would never be brought to light.

In Matthew 18:15-17, Christ taught His church how to handle an unrepentant brother, and it clashes head on with the "covenant of confidentiality" promoted by Promise Keepers:

> And if your brother sins, go and reprove him in private; if he listens to you, you have won your brother. But if he does not listen to you, take one or two more with you, so that by the mouth of two or three witnesses every fact may be confirmed. And if he refuses to listen to them, tell it to the church; and if he refuses to listen even to the church, let him be to you as a Gentile and a tax-gatherer (Matt. 18:15-17).

Suppose you employ Jack (a member of your church), and he has stolen from you by dipping into the cash register at work. He has sinned against you. Christ tells you in this passage to go to him privately to confront him with his sin (phase 1). If Jack tells you to get lost, you are to go back to him and take two or three witnesses—those who will witness the meeting and offer biblical counsel to both of you (phase 2). If Jack is indeed in the wrong and still refuses to listen, you must tell the matter to the church (phase 3), and if he still refuses to listen to the church, he must be put out of the church until he repents (phase 4).

But what if you followed the advice of the Promise Keepers by entering into a covenant of confidentiality with Jack in your small group? What now? You would never be able to obey Christ by moving beyond phase 1 or, perhaps, phase 2. In other words, *by promising to keep everything strictly confidential and keeping that covenant in the small group, you must disobey Christ who commands you tell the matter to the church.* Christ tells you to tell the church, but you have already promised that you would never tell anybody outside of the group.

Not only would the covenant of confidentiality, under these circumstances, put you in the position of disobeying Christ, it would also harm the very one it feigns to help— the offending brother—who needs others in the church to bring him to his senses. It would also harm the church which cannot take appropriate remedial action in the situation to safeguard the name of Christ. Thus, we should never promise anyone absolute confidentiality. To do so is to make a rash oath or vow which, as we saw in chapter six, is unbiblical. The most we can ever promise is that we will keep the matter as confidential as the Bible allows, and that we will involve others only if we are required by God to do so in obedience to Him.

Far from hindering us from becoming more Christlike as Gorsuch and Shaffer contend, refusing to enter into covenants of confidentiality honors Christ by honoring His Word. To become Christlike, we must obey Christ Himself. And if we want to obey Christ Himself, we will never put ourselves in the position of having to disobey Him downstream. But that is precisely what the covenant of confidentiality requires.

Were the Promise Keepers to disagree by arguing that Matthew 18:15-17 could be applied in the group itself, it would bring us full circle to one of our earlier criticisms: Promise Keepers moves from verses describing the church (the whole) to the small group (the part). While a small group may be part of a church, it is not a substitute for the church. Matthew 18 is addressed to the church, not to small groups. This is just one more way Promise Keepers unwittingly harms the local church in the name of helping it. Further, it should be obvious that if the small group were to handle the entire process of discipline, this means that the small group is claiming in fact to be the church.

The Family that Worships Together . . .

Another apparently innocuous way that Promise Keepers undermines the local church is its view of whether families should worship God together as families. One writer for *New Man*, Skip Burke, in an apparent attempt to be humorous, shows his cards when he writes that one of the eight ways parents can create "churchy kids" is to "(d)uct tape their squirming fannies to the pew, if that's what it takes, but keep your children in the adult service."[14] In other words, if you really want to turn your children off from church, require that they worship with you.

God has called *His people and their seed* (children) into a covenantal relationship with Him throughout Scripture (*e.g.* "For the promise is for you and your children . . ."—Acts 2:39). That is why classical Protestantism has always understood that the "visible church . . . consists of all those throughout the world that profess the true religion, *together with their children* . . ."[15]

Beyond that, both the Old and New Testaments teach us that children have consistently, so far as we can tell, participated in worship. In Joshua 8:30-35, for example, Israel worshipped God after the victory at Ai. Verses 33 and 35 tell us who was there: "All Israel with their elders and officers and their judges" including "the women and *the little ones* [toddlers] and the strangers who were living among them." This was no sermonette, either; the entire law of God was read (verse 34). In 2 Chronicles 20:1-19, after the Moabites and Ammonites invaded Judah, King Jehoshaphat called a day of fasting and prayer. Verse 13 tells us that "all Judah was standing before the Lord, with their *infants*, their wives, and their *children*." And older children are mentioned when Nehemiah 8:1-3 teaches us that men, women, and *"all who could listen with understanding* gathered together to hear the law read" (v. 2) in a service that lasted from early morning until midday (v. 3). Chronicles thus teaches us that when God's people gathered together to worship Him, infants and toddlers gathered with the adults, and Nehemiah shows us the presence of children capable of understanding.

Building upon this Old Testament pattern, the authors of the New Testament expected children to be present in worship. The epistles, for example, were written, in part, to be read during worship. Often, the epistles themselves specifically address children (*e.g.*, Eph. 6:1; Col. 3:20) who were obviously expected to be participating in the worship when these passages were read. Moreover, in the New Testament, as in the Old, entire households were baptized when the covenant head came to Christ (Acts 16:13-14; 27-34).

Admittedly, no one wants to create "churchy" kids, if by "churchy" we mean little legalists who run round after the service, all proud and conceited. But with all the promises made to children of believing parents, the doctrine of covenantal or generational succession taught throughout Scripture, and the specific examples of children worshipping God together with their families, we do not believe that our children need to be shipped off somewhere else during worship.

The Log in the Church's Eye

While the church certainly can point an accusing finger at the Promise Keepers movement, the Promise Keepers movement itself points an accusing finger right back at the church. The fact that Promise Keepers is perceived as necessary to reach men today is a sad commentary on the failure of the church. Had the church properly taught and discipled men to be godly men in all walks of life, the need for Promise Keepers would never have arisen. As one well-respected pastor and author frankly admitted, "The fact that [Promise Keepers] is such a felt need by so many confused people today is symptomatic of the abysmal failure of the church to be and do what Christ has commanded her to be and do!"[16]

But the church cannot be and do what Christ has commanded when she is filled with people who get mixed messages from movements like Promise Keepers about her role and importance in the life of the believer.

[1] *SPPK*, pp. 8, 129.

[2] "A Message to Pastors," *New Man*, November/December, 1995, vol. 2, no. 6, p. 86.

[3] *Ibid.*

[4] David Halbrook, quoting an anonymous pastor in "Pastors: Come to the Table," *New Man*, September/October, 1995, vol. 2, no. 5, p. 94.

[5] Horton, "What About the Promise Keepers Movement?", *The White Horse Inn* radio broadcast, tape no. WHI-237.

[6] Ken Canfield, "Treat Him Like a Best Friend," *New Man*, November/December, 1995, vol. 2, no. 6, p. 55.

[7] *Brothers!*, p. 12.

[8] *Ibid.*, p. 14.

[9] "Face to Face," *New Man*, September/October, 1995, vol. 2, no. 5, p. 54.

[10] *Ibid.*

[11] *Brothers!*, p. 16.

[12] *Ibid.*, p. 31.

[13] *Ibid.*, p. 51.

[14] Kip Burke, "Eight ways to Create Churchy Kids," July/August, 1995, vol.2, no. 4, p. 16.

[15] The Westminster Confession of Faith, Ch. 25, Sec. 2.

[16] G. I. Williamson, "A Look at Promise Keepers," *New Horizons*, January, 1996, p. 20.

❄ FOURTEEN ❄

Breaking Down the Walls—Promise 6

A Promise Keeper is committed to reaching beyond any racial and denominational barriers to demonstrate the power of biblical unity.[1]

In order to be right with anyone or anything else, men must first be right with God. In order to be biblically "unified" with others, we must first find unity and peace with God. But how can a man be right with God? This question is really at the heart of the Christian faith—the good news of the Christian message—which, as we have seen, addresses this question directly.

But this same question also reveals a significant problem with how Promise Keepers seeks to communicate this gospel message. In this chapter, we will look first at the gospel message itself, and then the problems this gospel message causes for the vision of racial and denominational unity sought by Promise Keepers in Promise 6.

Start Spreading the News

As Christians, we are called to spread the good news of the gospel. But what is that good news? We might classify two types of good news. The first is good news out of the blue—when one inherits an unexpected but vast fortune, for example. But the second kind of good news depends upon a previous understanding of some kind of bad news. The Greek word for gospel literally means "good news," but it is good news which falls in this second category. Just as a man cannot understand the good news of a governor's pardon if he does not understand himself to be on death row, so we cannot understand salvation from sin if we do not understand our own sinfulness. The Bible teaches that this understanding of sinfulness comes only from the law of God (Rom. 3:20; 5:20). The law is a perfect reflection of the character of a holy God—the God with whom we must be reconciled.

He is good, and we are not. In our own nature, we are dead in our trespasses and sins (Eph. 2:1-2). Apart from Christ's intervention, we are slaves to our sinfulness (Rom. 6:6). As natural men, we cannot even understand spiritual things (1 Cor. 2:14), much less trust in them for salvation. Paul teaches that the message of the cross is foolishness to those who are perishing. This is indeed a desperate situation. The cross is our only hope of salvation, and apart from Christ, that message is foolishness to us (1 Cor. 1:18). Without God and without hope in the world, our situation apart from God is utterly desperate. We need a Savior, and the Bible teaches that salvation is found in Jesus Christ alone.

Now the exact meaning of this word *alone* is very important. Not only does it mean that there are no Saviors *in addition to* Jesus Christ, it also means there are no Saviors *in combination with* Jesus Christ. As evangelical Christians, we reject the idea that salvation is found apart from Christ; our Lord is not one of four available Saviors. But also as evangelical Christians, we should reject the idea that Christ needs help in saving us since He alone is our salvation. Because Christ alone is our salvation, we can say that salvation is all of grace. And grace, by its very nature, does not combine at all with any human effort or work. As Paul put it, "And if by grace, then it is no longer of works; otherwise grace is no longer grace. But if it is of works, it is no longer grace; otherwise work is no longer work" (Rom. 11:6).

This is the biblical message. The grace found in Jesus Christ does not mix with anything else. The ground of our salvation is the person and work of Christ alone. Now as we look at church history, we see many attempts to subvert or twist this message so that it is no longer the biblical good news, the gospel message which saves.

Some such attempts at twisting the message have had more success in deception than others, and of course none of them has been completely honest in the advertising. No one comes to the front door, hands you a tract, and says, "Hello, I am here representing my father the devil, and I would like to share a false gospel with you." Rather, these subversions of the gospel have regularly come in the name of Christ. "For Satan himself transforms himself into an angel of light. Therefore it is no great thing if his ministers also transform themselves into ministers of righteousness, whose end will be according to their works" (2 Cor. 11:14-15).

As shown above, a doctrine central to the Christian faith is the truth that we are saved by faith, on the basis of the goodness of somebody else. Faith is the instrument of salvation, and the cross of Christ, its ground. To reverse this emphasis is to subvert the gospel. This reversal says we are saved by Jesus Christ on the basis of our faith. But the great Reformer, Martin Luther, said that the proper understanding of justification by faith alone is the mark of a standing or falling church. This issue, this point of division, was one of the central points of controversy in the Reformation of the sixteenth century. As a result of this controversy, the gospel was recovered, and clearly proclaimed by classical and orthodox Protestants. Are we saved on the basis of the goodness of Christ alone, received through the instrument of faith alone? Or are we saved by the goodness of Christ in combination with other efforts and decisions?

In the sixteenth century, the Roman Catholic church held an ecumenical council which is known as the Council of Trent. During this council, the Roman Catholic church unambiguously repudiated the gospel of justification by grace alone through faith alone on account of Christ alone. In fact, it pronounced anathemas on anyone who believed it: "If any one saith, that justifying faith is nothing else but confidence in the divine mercy which remits sins for Christ's sake; or, that this confidence alone is that whereby we are justified: let him be anathema [cursed, ed.]."[2]

The issue was whether or not the ground of our salvation is the righteousness of Christ alone, and whether or not we receive His righteousness by and through the instrument of faith alone. The ramifications of this doctrinal disagreement were and are immense. Nothing less was at stake than fidelity to the gospel itself. In the years since Trent, the Roman Catholic church has done nothing which modifies her horrifying repudiation of the gospel.

Properly understood, it was not the Protestants who separated themselves from the church, but rather, the Roman Catholic church which separated itself from the gospel and hence, from the church.

Unequally Yoked?

But what does all this have to do with Promise Keepers? Promise Keepers plays down the rift between Protestants and Catholics, treating it as unimportant. Jack Hayford, in *Seven Promises of a Promise Keeper*, for example, says, "Whether your tradition celebrates it as Communion, Eucharist, the Mass, or the Lord's Supper, we are all called to this centerpiece of Christian worship."[3] Hayford has reduced the centrality of the cross to a matter of personal preference: you may like chocolate, and I may like vanilla, but we all call it ice cream.

In an address at more than one Promise Keepers conference, the founder of Promise Keepers and former Roman

Catholic, Bill McCartney, said, "Now hear this. Promise Keepers doesn't care if you are a Catholic. Do you love Jesus? Are you born of the Spirit of God?"

Promise Keepers could not make these claims if it believed that the doctrinal issues traditionally separating Protestants from Catholics are central. This means that classical Protestants who still believe the gospel is central, are excluded from Promise Keepers based on the stand Promise Keepers has taken. In other words, unity is possible between Catholicism and Promise Keepers, but is impossible with convinced Protestants as long as Catholicism separates itself from gospel truth. We are not trying to strain at gnats here, but we must see that this is not a dispute over whether the choir should walk up the left or right aisle—this question concerns the very definition of what it means to be a Christian. However, Promise Keepers is treating the differences between Protestants and Catholics as just another "denominational" difference.

Even while we object to the false unity promoted by Promise Keepers, we are not maintaining that all Catholics are unregenerate. We are convinced that many members of that communion have been converted while in her midst. They are in good company. The same can be said of Wyclif, Hus, Luther, and Calvin, just to name a few. The issue is not *individual* Catholics, but rather, the formal stand taken by the institution of the Roman Catholic church itself, repudiating the gospel, and cursing those who understand and embrace it. Therefore, the duty of those Catholics who have come to saving faith is to leave that church as soon as they possibly can. Further, it is the duty of all confessing Protestants to encourage and aid them as they leave. The position taken by Promise Keepers is not merely that individual Catholics can be regenerate. If that were the issue, there would be no controversy. The problem is the formal position of the Catholic church, that of repudiating the gospel, and the formal position of Promise Keepers accepting that church as a Christian church regardless.

Given Promise Keepers' position, it is not surprising that Roman Catholic leaders have supported the movement wholeheartedly. Assuaging any possible fear that Promise Keepers is out to proselytize Roman Catholics, one priest in the Los Angeles area was recently quoted by *The Los Angeles Times* as saying that "Promise Keepers places a very strong emphasis on returning to your own church congregation or parish and becoming an active layman."[4] This same priest was previously quoted in the official newspaper of the Los Angeles Archdiocese, *The Tidings*, as commending Promise Keepers because "(t)here is no attempt at proselytizing or drawing men away from their faith to another church."[5] *The Tidings* thus endorsed the Promise Keepers movement and encouraged Roman Catholic men to attend the Los Angeles conference in 1995:

> Promise Keepers is a basic program of evangelization for men of faith, begun among more fundamentalist and evangelical Christian communities, but now being expanded to include Catholic congregations.[6]

Months earlier, Cardinal Roger Mahoney of the Archdiocese of Los Angeles, had written that he was "very interested to know how the Archdiocese of Los Angeles and I could be of assistance in the fuller promotion of Promise Keepers" and said that he "would be open to any suggestions . . . [regarding] an expansion of the Promise Keeper concept among our Catholic men."[7] Since then, Roman Catholics have been involved promoting Promise Keepers in many states. Quite a few of the many "Wake Up Calls" sponsored by Promise Keepers have featured Roman Catholic clergy as key speakers, as though the Roman Catholic church were just another denomination. Even then, however, Promise Keepers plays down denominational differences.

In the end, the official Promise Keepers position calls us to transcend and overlook the barriers between Catholics and Protestants. By so doing, Promise Keepers calls us to transcend and overlook the gospel.

The Heart of Reconciliation

The formal position of the Roman Catholic church on justification by faith alone is entirely at odds with the biblical position. Regardless of the personal standing of individual Catholics, the formal Catholic position must be formally rejected by any self-professing evangelical organization, movement, or institution. Through explicit statements, such as those given above, and the policy of accepting Catholics as simply members of "just another denomination," it seems clear that Promise Keepers as an institution is not willing to take the stand that doctrinal integrity requires.

At best, the stand Promise Keepers has taken is the result of doctrinal confusion. At worst, it is the result of conviction—a conviction that salvation by faith alone is a peripheral doctrine. In either case, whether it stems from a deep-seated confusion or an erroneous conviction, the men involved with Promise Keepers are effectively hindered in fulfilling Promise 1. Recall that Promise 1 speaks of "honoring Jesus Christ through worship, prayer, and obedience to God's Word"—the very thing Promise Keepers renders impossible by its own doctrinal compromise. Justification by faith alone is the heart of the gospel, and one of the central teachings of Scripture, and it is this truth which sets us free to study and understand the rest of God's Word. Not only is this gospel true, it is declared at the point where we enter into all truth. "Behold the proud, his soul is not upright within him; but the just shall live by his faith" (Hab. 2:4).

In order to obey the gospel, we must first understand it. "For the time has come for judgment to begin at the house of God; and if it begins with us first, what will be the end of those who do not obey the gospel of God?" (1 Pet. 4:17). Paul says something very similar when he refers to those who will be judged because they "do not obey the gospel of our Lord Jesus Christ" (2 Thess. 1:8). In Scripture, if we truly believe the gospel, we will obey the gospel.

But we cannot obey the gospel if we have not heard and understood it. As we showed earlier, a proper understanding of the gospel is not natural to the natural man. In order to understand the saving gospel, it must be declared faithfully, clearly, plainly, bluntly, and in the power of the Holy Spirit. "And how shall they hear without a preacher?" (Rom. 10:14).

Jesus Christ cannot be honored through a disobedient or confused approach to the knowledge of His Father. Because of Christ's perfect obedience, a sinner may come to the Father through the instrument of faith alone. But if he confuses the obedience of Christ with his own obedience through faith, then he has confused the difference between grace and works. And that confusion, the Bible tells us, is eternally fatal.

By blurring the central doctrine of justification by grace alone through faith alone on account of Christ alone, Promise Keepers has tragically obscured and confused the way to the Father. And because Promise Keepers' theology of vertical reconciliation with God is flawed, so is its theology of horizontal reconciliation with man. We will never be able to effect true horizontal reconciliation if we fail to understand true vertical reconciliation since the latter is the basis of the former. Without being reconciled to God by grace alone through faith alone on account of Christ alone, we can never be truly reconciled to one another.

The Black or White Fallacy

Earlier, we applauded Promise Keepers for assaulting the sin of racism. At the same time, we must qualify our applause—especially since we live in a politically correct age. Whenever attacking any sin becomes popular outside the church, we should all get more than a little nervous. Christ said that we should beware when all men think well of us, and presumably the same would apply when all men think well of our denunciations. Our responsibility as Christians is to *act* on the basis of what the Word says, and not *react* to whatever we see done around us. We must not react to those of other races, which is racism, but we must not react to the ever-present establishment visions of racism either. A ditch can always be found on either side of the road. The Bible identifies racism as a sin, and we are to be obedient at this point, whatever it costs. In Christ there is neither Jew nor Greek, slave or free, male or female (Gal. 3:28). This truth should be enough for us.

We must not take our cues from the world on this, and be misled by a formal similarity in terms. The fact that the world condemns racism, and the fact that the believing church does so also, does not mean that they are addressing the same problem. If we admit the fundamental tenets of political correctness, it will come back to haunt us. In our politically correct age, Paul would have gotten in trouble for his slam on Cretans—"liars, evil beasts, lazy gluttons" (Tit. 1:12). And Christ, of course, would have been rebuked for His insensitive comments regarding the blind leading the blind and all that (*e.g.*, Matt. 15:14). What He *really* meant was the visually challenged . . . .

We should not take our cues of what constitutes sin from popular American culture. By the same token, when we have identified a sin, we must be careful to deal with it as Scripture requires. Men are to repent of their sins, and where necessary, they are to make restitution. But biblical restitution requires careful and ample demonstration—not just popular slogans. The popular practice of dividing along color lines, and the groupthink it reveals, is honestly an evidence that the problems which cause racism are still very much with us.

The Bible teaches us there *is* a shared covenantal responsibility within families and within nations. But we find nothing about skin color, considered as such. We can illustrate the point by considering the case of the ancestors of American blacks, brought to America in the monstrous slave trade, what one theologian rightly called an "iniquitous traffick." Because this was such a great evil, does this mean that whites as whites owe restitution to blacks as blacks? The answer is *not at all*—although it would be nice if the situation were as simple as all that.

The blacks who were brought here were overwhelmingly enslaved in Africa by other blacks, taken down the coast, and sold to white traders. After some time here, in one of history's little quirks, some of the slaves were actually owned by free blacks, and in any event, the vast majority of whites did not own slaves. A horrible war was fought which muddled things still further. Complicating the analysis even more, the ancestors of many other modern American whites who showed up in America several centuries after the slaves first arrived, were themselves poorly received— *e.g.* the Irish.

Anyone who wants to make biblical restitution now on the basis of *nothing more than skin color* is simply ignorant of history. We would be confronted with the spectacle of a man whose grandfather arrived at Ellis Island in 1890 making restitution to a black man whose ancestors themselves owned slaves one hundred years earlier in New Orleans.

We favor the biblical approach of repentance and forgiveness for current sins, and restitution for past sins which can be shown to have a clear covenantal connection to us. Consequently, we would want to caution Promise Keepers that a great deal of discernment is needed on an issue such as this. When it comes to making restitution, more is required than simply saying that it is sinful to hate people on account of the color of their skin. So much is obvious, but many of our current problems are found in the details—details which we seem unable to face.

For example, in *New Man*, we are told that we must "Repent for [our] own and America's racist sins of the past."[8] We are also provided with examples of those who have done so as role models for the rest of us to follow. In one issue of *New Man*, Christian pop artist Steve Green confessed "I felt it was my Christian responsibility to ask forgiveness on behalf of my race and those who wounded Larnelle [Harris] . . ."[9]

While those who are racists *do* need to ask forgiveness of those to whom they vented their hatred, what Green has done and what Promise Keepers encourages is what we call "reparational reconciliation"—asking forgiveness for the sins of others in the past. There are some serious biblical concerns with this practice. First, where in the Bible are we ever told to ask forgiveness for a sin we did not commit and for which we are not covenantally responsible? Look long and hard and you will find nothing like it in the Bible. Second, reparational reconciliation ends up promoting the very tokenism that lies at the heart of racism—treating someone differently on account of the color of his skin. Third, some in our society have no responsibility for the injustices perpetrated against those of other races since their relatives had absolutely no involvement in the "iniquitous traffick." Fourth, why stop with whites seeking reparational reconciliation with non-whites? Why not have men ask forgiveness of women on behalf of all men? Or three tall men ask forgiveness from all short guys? Or white collar workers from blue collar workers? Or pretty women from plain women? Where do we stop?

If someone has wronged a person of another race or denomination, he can't seek forgiveness from *another* member of that race or denomination. It doesn't work that way. The sin was against a particular person. Forgiveness doesn't work with tokens, and these substitutionary voodoo apologies do far more harm than good. Unless there is some covenantal connection or responsibility for the sins others have committed, then to assume arbitrary responsibility is simply impudence. One cannot seek forgiveness on behalf of some-body else if he has no covenantal responsibility for that somebody else.

Sin Not Skin, Grace Not Race

Those from whom the forgiveness is sought often real-ize that nothing is really being accomplished by it. It is no-cost forgiveness, and no-effect restitution. For example, *New Man* reported that some young blacks at a recent NAACP convention bucked the modern wisdom when, in July of 1994, they told their "elders" to stop complaining about the evils of white society. One participant at that conference was quoted as saying "We can't blame another race for our problems. The new generation of black youth wants to stop blaming the white society. It's up to us to change."[10] Racists should stop hating others on account of the color of their skin, but "victims" need to stop blaming the system. Unfor-tunately, Promise Keepers rhetoric plays into the victim mentality.

The problem is worsened when Promise Keepers applies verses to this problem which have nothing to do with racial reconciliation. Promise Keepers president, Randy Phillips, once wrote that ". . . the biblical directive to pursue recon-ciliation compels Promise Keepers to address the division that has separated the body of Christ for too long (Jn. 17:20-23; 2 Cor. 5:18-19)."[11] John 17 does address the unity of the body of Christ, but 2 Corinthians 5 addresses the enmity and alienation of unbelievers from God. 2 Corinthians 5 has nothing to do with enmity in the body of Christ. The "min-istry of reconciliation" Paul speaks of in that chapter is a ministry of reconciling those who are estranged from God as unbelievers. This is bad exegesis and bad theology. Racial hostility is lamentable, but we must address it in the way

Scripture requires. This means getting the gospel straight, and then *preaching* it. In *Christ*, there is neither Jew nor Greek, slave nor free, male nor female (Gal. 3:28). So right was Bishop Phillip Porter, chairman of the board of Promise Keepers, when he proclaimed that sin, not skin, is the problem, and grace, not race, the solution.[12]

Questions About Unity

We began this chapter with a discussion of the nature of the gospel—the only possible foundation for biblical unity. Contrasted with this is the humanistic desire for unity—"c'mon, people now, smile on your brother"—which appears to be based on nothing more than our common humanity. Obviously, blacks and whites, Catholics and Protestants, evangelicals and Rotary Club members all share a common humanity. Consequently, the law of God requires that we treat one another as created in the image of God. But treating one another with the dignity which a common humanity requires, and treating one another as brothers in Christ are two entirely different things. The first is based upon the authority of God over creation, while the second is based upon the truth revealed in Christ in redemption.

Now Promise Keepers has clearly fallen into the trap of accepting a blurred humanistic vision of unity, rather than the unity *in Christ* which the Bible sets before us. This can be seen in how this year's theme of "Break Down the Walls" is being promoted. As one Promise Keeper letter put it, the enemy which we must overcome is "racial and denominational distrust." The language of Promise 6 is very similar. We are to reach past any "racial and denominational barriers" in order to achieve unity. Clearly, racial and denominational differences are being lumped together, and we are urged to overcome them in the same way. But racial differences are God-given and part of His creation design, while denomi-

national differences are the result of our sinfulness, igno-
rance, and shortsightedness.

Racial harmony is achieved when we learn to accept
Christian brothers the way God made them. Denominational
differences are to be reconciled by coming together to study
the Scriptures (Acts 17:11), in a spirit that is willing to strive
for "likemindedness" (Rom. 15:5; Phil. 2:2,20). Where denominational differences exist, they are to be removed as a
result of one side, or the other, or both, *changing* in order to
submit to the teaching of Scripture. We must affirm racial
differences; we must never affirm our sinful disagreements.
Doctrinal differences can and should be resolved through
Bible study. But you could study the Bible until you turned
blue, and that wouldn't change your color . . . well, you
know what we mean. Until we arrive at likemindedness, we
should certainly not be disagreeable. And if this were all
that Promise Keepers meant in Promise 6, there would be
no difficulty. But much more is involved: the authority of
truth.

This principle, as with so much else, *is* acknowledged at
some points by some representatives of Promise Keepers.
For example, Promise Keepers Vice President of Ministry
Advancement, E. Glenn Wagner admits that "unity is not a
oneness at the expense of the truth."[13] He even goes as far as
quoting the accomplished Bible commentator, William
Hendriksen, who, in expositing Christ's prayer for unity in
John 17, wrote, "Believers, therefore, should always yearn
for peace, but never for peace at the expense of truth, for
unity which has been gained by means of such a sacrifice is
not worthy of the name."[14] This is wonderfully stated. In
this same book, Wagner goes still further by saying, "Unity
is not an ecumenical endeavor to find the lowest common
denominator among people even if it means denying cardinal doctrines such as the deity of Christ or the inerrancy of
the Scriptures."[15] Amen.

But the practical application of this concept by Promise

Keepers is quite different. Elsewhere, in the very same book, unity is described as ultimately being a matter of *relationship*. Unity is "being in relationship to one another."[16] "It is this idea of relationship that will bring us into unity."[17] No. It is truth that unites. It is truth that results in our relationships with one another in the body of Christ. It is the truth of the gospel that makes us brothers in the first place. We know certain facts to be true—that we are sinners, that Christ lived a life of perfect obedience for us and died in our place, that He rose again; we assent to or agree with those truths; and we trust in them for our salvation. Then, we are brought into relationship with one another. We can have no true fellowship with those who part from the core truths of the faith. Relationship is the result of unity, not the other way around.

Wagner argues that doctrine divides truth from error and unites us around the truth.[18] He then gives the example of a friend who believes that we can be saved based on our good works and shows how he cannot be unified with him in this belief. We concur, but hasn't Wagner just contradicted the official Promise Keepers stance on fellowship with those who deny the doctrine of justification? On the one hand, Promise Keepers has affirmed the fundamentals of the faith, but on the other, they have stated that we must overcome denominational barriers—barriers which were created by a denial of these fundamentals. If Roman Catholicism is considered just another denomination, then this emphasis on primary truths is inconsistent. And if the truth on the primaries of the gospel cannot be compromised, then the stance toward Roman Catholicism is inconsistent. Promise Keepers cannot have it both ways.

Part of the problem regarding the Promise Keepers stand on unity stems from a misunderstanding of Matthew 18:15-17. Says Wagner,

> If someone disagrees with us in one of the five fundamentals [the doctrines of Scripture, God, Christ, the Holy

Spirit, and Redemption] Matthew 18 comes into play. The
so-called believer who does not hold to the truth is committing sin—specifically the sin of heresy—and therefore
he or she must be put out of the local church fellowship
and/or the denomination."[19]

But can Wagner truly say that the Roman Catholic Church
adheres to the five essentials as Promise Keepers has defined
them in *The Awesome Power of Shared Beliefs*? We have a problem here. If Promise Keepers truly believes that the five truths
articulated in *The Awesome Power of Shared Beliefs* are the
dividing line, then it has acted inconsistently with that dividing line.

As we see it, Promise Keepers wanted to have an official
position it could "point to" in order to calm the fears of
those who believed it was compromising the gospel. So it
sanctioned *The Awesome Power of Shared Beliefs*. But then
the movement still continues to work with institutions that
are avowed enemies of the gospel as defined in that book.
Promise Keepers now has the best of both worlds. They
have an answer for every critic—with one exception: the critic
who points out inconsistencies. If the dividing line is as announced in *The Awesome Power of Shared Beliefs*, then it must
be enforced across the board and down the line. If not, Promise Keepers must say so.

Drawing the Line

The problems caused by this type of compromise are
not going to stop at the differences between Catholics and
Protestants. Principles, or lack of them, can be applied in
any number of situations. During the Promise Keepers 1995
conference in Los Angeles, the *Los Angeles Times* reported
that "because of Promise Keepers' interdenominational approach, attorney Chip Rawlings and fellow Mormon leaders . . . are urging members of the Latter-day Saints to par-

ticipate in the movement." Why? Because according to Rawlings, "The movement's 'Seven Promises' are like something straight out of the men's priesthood manual for the [Mormon] church."[20] Earning one's salvation is evidently a crowd pleaser. The only question is whether it pleases God.

We wholeheartedly agree that Christians are not to squabble and fight over whether we should baptize with heads upstream or downstream. An emphasis on truth includes the truth that Christians are to love the peace of Christ's kingdom, and are to maintain a sense of biblical priorities. As Wagner himself put it,

> We must be careful not to call people to an inferior cause. We need to stop championing causes that are divisive to the body; instead we must call people to a unifying cause, which is the proclamation of the gospel and the expansion of the kingdom.[21]

Absolutely.

But what *is* the gospel? And what is involved in the expansion of His kingdom? Do we shy away from controversy, say, over the deity of Christ, for example, because we might offend those, like the Mormons, who claim to be in the body of Christ but who deny that doctrine? Do we shy away from the doctrine of the Trinity? If not, why not? The answer is that we must speak where Scripture speaks. But if we must speak where Scripture speaks, then we must make sure that we are speaking *everywhere* Scripture speaks. We must not shrink from declaring the whole counsel of God, as Paul says in Acts 20:27. True integrity demands nothing less.

Besides, who is divisive? Those who teach false doctrine as gospel truth or those who correct false gospel with gospel truth? The answer which Scripture gives is the former, not the latter. If the heretic or errant brother can claim a soapbox why can't the true believer correct him in love? Isn't that what Priscilla and Aquilla did with Apollos? Even though he was "mighty in the Scriptures," he needed to be taken aside and have the way of God explained to him more accurately. Paul, too, was divisive when he corrected Peter and Barnabas in their hypocrisy. The bottom line is that doctrine divides. It divides truth from error. Ideas have consequences. If you have the idea that you need to save yourself by what *you* do, it could have devastating eternal consequences. Someone who loves you would make it an issue.

Christians in times past unified around what they believed. Now we are called to unify around a common experience that we can share with thousands of others who may not believe that Christ is the only hope of salvation. What kind of unity is this, really? We do not believe it is the unity commended to us in the Bible. Unfortunately, Promise 6 requires us to blur certain distinctions which Scripture requires us to keep sharp.

In the end, those who refuse to embrace the true gospel are the ones who have separated themselves from the body of Christ. *They* are the ones who need to repent. *They* are the ones who need to be reconciled—first to God, and then, to their brothers, whether they be black, yellow, red or white. The only reconciliation possible is on the rock solid foundation of the gospel. Any other foundation is sinking sand.

---

[1] *SPPK*, p. 8, 153.

[2] Philip Schaff, *The Creeds of Christendom*, vol. 2 (Grand Rapids, MI: Baker Book House, 1990), p. 113.

[3] *SPPK*, p. 19.

[4] Christian Van Liefde, quoted in John Dart, "'Promise Keepers,' a Message to L.A. Men," *Los Angeles Times*, May 6, 1995, p. B4.

[5] Mike Nelson, "'Promise Keepers' Promises Spiritual Renewal for Men," *The Tidings*, March 31, 1995, p. 3, quoted in James Albert Dager, "Promise Keepers Update: Mormons, Catholics Laud Men's

Movement, *Media Spotlight*, vol. 16, no. 1, p. 1.

[6] *Ibid.*

[7] Letter quoted in "Promise Keepers Update: Mormons, Catholics Laud Men's Movement, *Media Spotlight*, vol. 16, no. 1, p. 1.

[8] Louis Priebe, "10 Steps for Unity," *New Man*, September/October, 1995, vol. 2, no. 5, p. 12.

[9] David Halbrook, "The Healing Power of Forgiveness," September/October, 1994, vol. 1, no. 2, p. 59.

[10] Anon., "Pointing Fingers," *New Man*, November/December, 1994, vol. 1, no. 3, p. 15.

[11] *New Man*, November/December, 1994, vol. 1, no. 3, p. 70.

[12] Press Conference, Dallas, Texas, October 27, 1995.

[13] *TAPSB*, p. 22.

[14] Quoted in *TAPSB*, p. 25.

[15] *TAPSB*, p. 22.

[16] *Ibid.*, p. 23.

[17] *Ibid.*, p. 11.

[18] *Ibid.*, pp. 34-35.

[19] *Ibid.*, p. 180.

[20] Dart, John, "Promise Keepers, a Message to L.A. Men," *Los Angeles Times*, May 6, 1995, p. B13.

[21] *TAPSB*, p. 9.

❈ FIFTEEN ❈

The Great Omission—Promise 7

A Promise Keeper is committed to influencing his world, being obedient to the Great Commandment (see Mark 12:30-31) and the Great Commission (see Matt. 28:19-20).[1]

When our Lord stood on the mount, about to ascend to the right hand of the Father, His disciples, sensing His imminent departure, anxiously asked Him when He would restore the kingdom to Israel (Acts 1:6). Instead of indulging their end-times inquiry, He told them that it was of no concern to them *when* God had ordained such things to take place, only *that* they would take place. Far more important than probing the secret will of the Father was the obedience they were to render to His revealed will (v. 7). In particular, He told them to be His witnesses in Jerusalem, Judea, Samaria, and even to the remotest part of the earth (v. 8).

As He began to ascend, the disciples, quite naturally, were riveted on Him the whole way, even well after He was out of sight. Suddenly, two angels appeared and, almost scoldingly, asked them why they were spending their time gazing intently into the sky when they had just been given their marching orders.

What a lesson for us all! Christianity is not a pie-in-the-sky faith. It is a roll-up-the-sleeves-faith, calling on those who embrace it to set about doing what they have been commanded to do by their risen Lord. No doubt, an important part of the obedience we are to render to Him involves bearing witness for Him in our small corner of the earth.

But we shouldn't unnecessarily limit our understanding of what it means to bear witness for Him to handing out tracts, going door-to-door, or standing on a soapbox. When it comes to the Great Commission, the church is sometimes guilty of what we call the Great Omission—the tendency to omit the many ways believers are called to bear witness for Him.

At times, even Promise Keepers falls prey to this tendency, especially when it comes to one of the most powerful, but perhaps most overlooked, means of bearing witness for Christ—that of our vocational callings. All of life, including our vocations, is a calling from God and is to bear witness for Him.

The Priorities Game

With a few exceptions, Promise Keepers unduly minimizes the witness-bearing impact of our vocational callings, usually by relegating those callings to the bottom rung of the ladder and placing God or the family at the top rung. God is first, family, second, and work, third, we are told. We call this ordering the priorities game, and we find it throughout Promise Keepers literature.

The God-over-job ordering appears frequently. As just one illustration, consider what Stu Weber has written in *New Man*. Pondering the fact that man was made for a cause, something outside of himself and beyond, Weber denigrates what he calls our "puny jobs" and sets them over against God:

> If you and I keep trying to attach our purpose for living to some work-a-day profession or 9-to-5 job, we forfeit the heart of true masculinity. No wonder so many of us become frustrated in our careers and find ourselves on the

canyon's rim of life crises. No wonder we find ourselves numbed at times by the crushing emptiness of it all. We're looking for a purpose, and it doesn't lie within our puny jobs . . .

We must find that purpose outside of ourselves. We must find it in Him.[2]

Weber's advice sounds good and pious on the surface. The problem with it, however, is that it fails to recognize that all of life is a calling from God, including what we do from 9-to-5. While our vocational calling should never become our *only* "purpose for living," it nevertheless is *one of our many* purposes for living. Nowhere in Scripture are we ever called to look away from our jobs to God. It's not that simple. We are to look *through* our jobs *to* God. God made us to glorify and enjoy Him, and one of the ways we do so is by serving Him in and through our jobs. The dualism inherent in Weber's comments is patently unbiblical.

All in the Family?

While Weber places God-over-job, other Promise Keepers authors place family-over-job. One reviewer for *New Man*, for instance, commended a soundtrack entitled "Promise Keepers: A Life that Shows," because it promoted "choosing family over career."[3] Gary Smalley assures his male readers that "when you decide to put your wife (and kids) above everything else on earth, you at once plant the seeds of security and hope."[4] *New Man* also lauded former Atlanta Braves pitcher, Tim Burke, after he gave up his career as a baseball player for his family. As it turns out, Burke was the first inductee into the "Fatherhood Hall of Fame" sponsored by the National Fatherhood Initiative whose director, Wade Horn, honored Burke by saying: "The way Tim Burke is living his life is a perfect example of how we expect fathers to treat their children."[5]

With all due respect to Mr. Horn, and assuming that Burke had good reasons for doing what he did, it is nevertheless strange to hold him up as an example for other fathers to follow. Burke made hundreds of thousands of dollars per year playing baseball and obviously had more choices available to him than the average father struggling to pay his mortgage and feed his family. While there may very well be men out there who need to change career paths because those career paths prevent them from fulfilling their calling as husbands and fathers, there is something strange about making the extraordinary example of Burke the example for the rest of us ordinary folk to follow.

But even more fundamentally, are we really called by God to give first place honors to family and just honorable mention to our vocations? Where is this priority scheme taught in Scripture? Isn't all of life a calling from God? Isn't Christ Lord of all? Shouldn't we simply view our marriages, families, and vocations as different aspects of our life-calling from God? Isn't "choosing family over career" a false dilemma? And what does it really mean to "put your wife (and kids) above all else on earth"? Does that mean that the day your colleagues at work are depending upon you to complete an important assignment, but your wife and kids ask you to stay home and go shopping, that you pile the clan in the Suburban and head for the mall? If not, then what does it mean?

At times, Promise Keepers seemingly strikes a better balance. Bill McCartney, for example, comes a little closer to the biblical equilibrium when he challenges men by telling them that "no amount of success at work can take the place of failure at home."[6] And Promise Keepers author, H.B. London Jr., did well to quote former U.S. Senate chaplain, Richard Halverson, who wrote of

> the man who has become a whale of a success downtown and a pathetic failure at home. He's a big shot with the

boys in the office and a big phony with the boys at home. He's a status symbol in society and a fake with the family.[7]

Admittedly, some men need to sit up and heed this somber warning. But we shouldn't forget that the reverse is also true. Success in the suburbs never excuses failure downtown. Your client facing a multi-million dollar judgment would take little, if any, comfort in knowing that you could have prepared a better defense of his case but instead sloughed off your professional responsibilities because you chose to go fly fishing with your boys the week before his trial got underway. And few patients about to go under the knife would be relieved to know that their surgeon thought of his calling as a "puny job" but really had a well adjusted spouse and children at home. Three cheers for a happy home! But please, not at the expense of one's vocational calling.

Another author was right on target when he encouraged readers to look at the different aspects of a man's life as spokes on a wheel, each of which must be balanced if the wheel is ever going to start rolling. He writes: "Though it is often discussed, there is no place in the Bible that teaches a 1-2-3 hierarchy of priorities. In fact, such an approach may cause more problems than it solves."[8] He is absolutely right, not just logistically, but theologically, as well.

But comments like this one are rare in the Promise Keeper literature. Ususally we see the various aspects of our lives ranked, as though they were in a foot race with one another. But when they are in competition, how do we determine the winner?

Usually the criterion is *time*—how much time do you spend on these various activities? But this criterion is not scriptural. If a man spends eight hours at work and one hour with his son, this does not mean he loves his job eight times more than he loves his son. Rather we should ask whether we are doing what the Bible requires of us in each aspect of our calling. This includes marriage, children, church, and *work*. Seeking first the kingdom of God involves serving and glorifying Him in every aspect of our lives.

Who's on First?

Why should we ultimately refuse to play the priorities game? Because Christ is Lord of all and as Lord, He demands that we serve Him in all of life. We need to strive for biblical balance by looking at the different aspects of life and giving each what Scripture determines to be its due, along with the rest. More than two hundred years ago, one pastor wisely cautioned his readers that they ought to order their "affairs relating to heaven and earth, to God and [their] family that they may not interfere or cross each other."[9] He goes on to observe that the "faithful and wise steward will give every one their portion, their meat in due season; as he will give his body and his family their portion every day, so he will give God and his soul their portion every day."[10] He is then quick to add that "there is a time for all things" such that we do "not so much as want time as waste time."[11]

What is so refreshing about this view is its balance in avoiding the priorities game. The biblically balanced view is that each aspect of our calling is to receive its due. To use the wise pastor's own metaphor, just like you feed each of your children every day, so you need to feed each aspect of your life every day. You shouldn't starve one to feed the other or vice versa.

But notice the pastor's pointed conclusion that "there is a time for all things" such that we do "not so much as want time as waste time." Isn't that the real issue when it comes to balancing the various aspects of our lives? The real problem with most men is not that they work too much. It's not what they do at the office that results in neglecting their wives and children. It's what they do, and what they refuse to do, when they get home.

Curt Swindoll, son of popular evangelical writer and speaker, Charles Swindoll, learned this lesson the hard way having grown up with a dad who was pulled in so many different directions. In a rather candid interview with *New Man*, he insightfully noted that the problem may really be how men use their leisure time:

> This [spending time with the family] isn't only about the salesman who spends 40 weeks a year on the road. This would include dads who come home from work and instantly turn on the TV or pick up the newspaper. They're missing out on spending time with their kids. Someday they're going to regret it.[12]

What the younger Swindoll is getting at intuitively is absolutely true and factually verifiable. For most men, what separates them from their families is *not their work*, but their use of leisure time. Sure leisure time is a good thing, but not when it is abused. Watching television for three hours every night is not the way to spend time with your family. Did you know that for every twenty-four hour period, men, on average, spend seven hours and ten minutes working and five hours and thirty minutes on leisure activities.[13] Put differently, men, on average, spend only an hour and a half more at work than they do at play. Now, we ask you, do you want time or waste it? That is the question of the hour, and that is where the real tension with the family comes into play.

The biblical balance is discovered when we remember that the Christian life is an integrated whole under the Lordship of Christ. It should not be artificially broken up into first or second or third place compartments which have little or nothing to do with one another. As Christians, we are called to glorify God in all that we do—even in otherwise mundane "secular" activities like eating and drinking (1 Cor. 10:31). Whatever we do, we are to do it in His name giving thanks through Him to the glory of God the Father (Col.

3:17). Simply put, we are to live for the Lord (Rom. 14:7-8).

If all of the Christian's life is to be lived as an integrated whole to the glory of God, we cannot treat some areas of life as though they were less important or less dignified than others in the eyes of God. But that is precisely what those who play the priorities game do. They fail to see that their entire lives constitute their calling from God, and instead absolutize one part of their lives, exalting it above the rest. Some go as far as idolizing part of their lives.

The net result is that far too many Christians fail to view their vocations as vehicles through which God will do His work through them as His royal priests (1 Pet. 2:9; Rev. 5:9). Believers are endowed with the incredible privilege of ministering for God daily wherever He has called them. But because some believers lose sight of their priestly calling, they slosh through their tasks day after day, week after week, losing valuable opportunities to serve God and glorify Him as priests in their vocations.

Learning on the Job

Some play the priorities game because they mistakenly have concluded that work is the result of the Fall. Accordingly, they have taken an unbiblically low view of work. But work is not a post-Fall institution. God put Adam in the Garden of Eden to be its caretaker (Gen. 2:15) *before* the Fall. He also commanded Adam to "subdue" the earth and to "rule" over creation (Gen. 1:27-28) before the Fall. Lest anyone forget, Genesis 1 and 2 come before Genesis 3! To be sure, God's curse upon Adam encompassed his work; he would have to toil all the days of his life (Gen. 3:17-19). But even then, *the curse, properly understood, affected only the circumstances surrounding his work, not the institution of work itself* (Gen 5:29). Adam worked before the Fall, and he would have to work thereafter. The only difference is that in the post-Fall world, he would have to work a little harder and sweat a little more.

While those who take an unbiblically low view of work forget that God ordained man to labor before the Fall, they also forget the high view of work found in Scripture even after the Fall. The fourth commandment as found in Exodus 20:8-11 and Deuteronomy 5:12-15, for example, commands us to work ("six days shalt thou labor and do all thy work") every bit as much as it commands us to rest ("in it [the sabbath] thou shalt not do any work"). It is no accident that believers who scorn the Lord's Day frequently end up scorning work and vice versa. Somewhat ironically, those who scorn the Lord's Day often end up resting six days a week and working on the seventh!

In addition to the fourth commandment, Scripture's high view of work can also be found in the many proverbs which both extol industriousness or diligence and condemn slothfulness or laziness (e.g., Prov. 10:4-5,26; 12:11,24,27; 13:4; 14:23; 19:15, 24; 20:4; 21:5,25; 22:13; 24:30-34; 26:13-16; Eccl. 9:10). Add to this list Solomon's timeless insight that we are to enjoy ourselves in our labor as well as the fruit of such labor since they are gifts from God and His reward to us (Eccl. 5:18-20).

And then there are Paul's injunctions to do our work to please the Lord (Eph. 6:5-8; Col. 3:22-24), to refrain from being busybodies and to work quietly for our own bread (1 Thess. 4:11-12; 2 Thess. 3:7-12), to labor for ourselves and those in need (Eph. 4:28), and to provide for those under our care lest we deny the faith and prove ourselves to be worse than unbelievers (1 Tim. 5:8,13-16).

From cover to cover, then, Scripture frowns on the notion that work is a post-Fall thing of drudgery. It is a pre-Fall institution which, even after the Fall, is both commanded and commended in Scripture. If even slaves are to do their work heartily as for the Lord (Eph. 6:5-8; Col. 3:22-24), we have no excuse. Their chains were real. Ours are only imaginary.

Still other Christians play the priorities game because they view their jobs simply as mission fields—going so far as to spend company time to witness to unbelieving colleagues or patrons, all the while thwarting their witness and quite possibly, harming their business in the process.

The bottom line is that, as our wise pastor told us, God has given us enough time to do everything He has called us to do. If you feel compelled to witness on company time, you should make up that time which rightfully belongs to your employer. The Lord, after all, never calls His priests to steal time from their employers (Ex. 20:15; Rom. 3:8).

We ought not to think that we are slighting God when we put our minds to our work. In fact, we slight God when we don't put our minds to our work since we are to serve and glorify Him through our work. The problem, as Os Guinness has correctly observed somewhere, is not that most Christians are not *where* they ought to be. It is that most Christians are not *what* they ought to be *where* they are. They are not serving and glorifying God as His priests in the workplace. In the words of Paul, they are not working "heartily, as for the Lord rather than men." Somewhere along the way, they have forgotten that it is "the Lord whom [they] serve" (Col. 3:23-24).

Those who have forgotten whom they serve in the workplace need to drink deeply from the well of the Reformers and their heirs on this point. Luther, for example, wrote that what seem to us to be "secular" works actually praise God and represent an obedience with which God is well-pleased. "There are no limits at all," he continues, "to this idea of calling. Wherever you are, whatever you are doing, you are able to please God in a concrete way and glorify His name and witness to Him by working."[14] Thus, we should not primarily work to witness in the narrow sense, but rather, should primarily witness in the broad sense through our work. Only then can we offer a powerful witness which will honor God, please Him, and truly glorify His holy name.

Answering the Call

No more sloshing. No more pious excuses. We should begin today to seize the opportunities God has given us. We should commit ourselves to pursue our respective vocations with vigor and zeal, without apology viewing them as opportunities to serve and glorify our great High Priest. We are not just Christians who happen to be plumbers, executives, or professors. We are called to be *Christian* plumbers, executives, and professors. We are not just Christians on Sunday. We are called to be Christians every day, including Monday through Friday. We are not just Christians at home. We are called to be Christians everywhere, including the workplace.

Seen in this light, our callings are not mere occupations—ways of occupying us or passing time until we can get home to spend the "most important" time of the day. Our callings are vocations, that is, callings from God by and through which we serve and glorify Him. Humbly recognizing the tremendous privilege God has bestowed on us through our great high priest, we should begin today to view our legitimate vocations—no matter what they may be—as one sphere of life through which we are to exercise our divinely ordained priesthood.

But many Christians head south precisely at this point by thinking that if their vocations don't overtly promote the Christian cause, they are somehow letting God down or failing to fulfill His calling or will in their lives. They fail to see that if they function as His priests by fulfilling His call in their lives, they *already* are promoting the Christian cause. They don't need to be doing "religious" things full-time to glorify God.

According to Luther, the work of the ministry, in the sight of God, is "in no way superior to the works of the farmer laboring in the field, or of a woman looking after her home."[15] And William Tyndale made the same point when he observed that in God's eyes there is no difference between washing dishes and preaching the gospel.[16] How's that for bringing the truth home? How's that for refusing to sell out to the priorities game?

The real distinction is not the time we spend in the corner office versus the family room. The real distinction is whether we are striving to glorify Christ by serving Him in each aspect of our calling. Ultimately, the real distinction is Christ. As one writer correctly noted:

> The only real farmer is a Christian farmer; the only real doctor is a Christian doctor; the only real man is a Christian man; and the only real woman is a Christian woman; and so on covering every detail and aspect and station in life. Apart from Christ we are not what we ought to be.[17]

Apart from Christ, we are nobody and can do nothing (Jn. 15:5). But by His grace, we are somebody and can do everything He calls us to do (Phil. 4:13).

Thus, "being all you can be" doesn't happen in any particular vocation as compared to another. Nor does it happen inside the home as opposed to outside it. Being all you can be comes as a direct result of being a Christian, of knowing Jesus Christ, and doing what He has called you to do. Understanding our vocations as callings from God should not only focus us inwardly to serve and glorify God as we vigorously pursue our respective vocations. It should also focus us outwardly to let our light so shine before men everywhere, even in the workplace, so that they, too, can become somebody—children of God—and glorify their Father in heaven (Matt. 5:16).

What Goes Around . . .

We have come full circle. We started with the laudable goal of Promise Keepers in Promise 7 to bear witness for

Christ but saw how, by playing the priorities game, it stifles one of the most effective means of bearing witness for Him: our vocational callings.

Yet if we obey Him in our vocational callings, seeking to glorify and enjoy Him in them, we will bear powerful testimony to Him. That's a message our world needs to hear but can only hear when we stop viewing the home as our only or primary mission field.

---

[1] *SPPK*, pp. 8, 181.

[2] "The Ultimate Tender Warrior," July/August, 1994, vol. 1, no. 1, p. 80, exerpted from *the Tender Warrior* (Multnomah, OR: Multnomah Books, Questar Publishers, 1993).

[3] David Halbrook, "The Latest from Promise Keepers," *New Man*, September/October, 1994, vol. 1, no. 2, p. 72.

[4] "Treat Her Like a Queen," *New Man*, January/February, 1996, vol. 3, no. 1, p. 33.

[5] Quoted in "Major League Dad," *New Man*, September/October, 1994, vol. 1, no. 2, p. 14.

[6] Press Conference, Dallas, Texas, October 27, 1995.

[7] Quoted in *SPPK*, p. 150.

[8] Michael A. Bechtle, "Wheel of Priorities," *New Man*, May/June, 1995, p. 72.

[9] *The Christian Man's Calling* (Edinburgh, Scotland: The Banner of Truth Trust, 1992 [1868]), pp. 307-308.

[10] *Ibid.*, pp. 309-310.

[11] *Ibid.*, p. 310.

[12] Julian Lukins, "Swindoll and Sons: Advice for Fathers," (Interview), *New Man*, January/February, 1996, vol. 3, no. 1, p. 28.

[13] Greg Johnson and Mike Yorkey," *Daddy's Home* (Wheaton, IL: Tyndale House Publishers, Inc., 1992), p. 52.

[14] Luther's Commentary on Genesis 3:13 as quoted by Alister McGrath, "The Protestant Work Ethic," (taped lecture) (Anaheim, CA: Christians United for Reformation, 1993).

[15] Quoted in Leland Ryken, *Worldly Saints: The Puritans as They Really Were* (Grand Rapids, MI: Academie Books, 1986), p. 228, note 3, citing W. R. Forester, *Christian Vocation* (New York, NY: Scribner, 1953), p. 148.

[16] William Tyndale in *The Parable of the Wicked Mammon*, quoted in Leland Ryken, *Worldly Saints*, p. 25.

[17] John Barkley, quoted in Cyril Eastwood, *The Priesthood of All Believers: An Examination of the Doctrine from the Reformation to the Present Day* (London, England: Epworth Press, 1960), p. 73.

Part Four:
Beyond Promises

✹ CONCLUSION ✹

Up for the Challenge

In 1995, Promise Keepers challenged men from coast to coast to "raise the standard" in their lives. As a slogan, "raise the standard" is somewhat ambiguous. It can imply that the standard is set by the individual trying to measure up to it. Yet it also can imply that the standard already has been set by another, although we simply need to do more on our end to measure up.

As Christians, however, we believe that there is only one standard: God, in Christ, as He has revealed Himself in Scripture. And since Scripture reflects the perfect holiness of God, it alone holds before us the perfect standard of holiness He requires of us as His people. Scripture tells us that we are to be perfect as He is perfect, to be holy for He is holy, to imitate Him. The standard cannot be raised. It already is as high as God is infinite. Our problem, then, is not that we have failed to raise the already infinite standard set before us, but that we have fallen far short of that standard. We *have not* because we *cannot*. We have not measured up to the infinite standard of God's perfect holiness because we cannot do so, and to make matters worse, we cannot pay the price required of us for our failure to measure up to that standard.

But the good news is that the infinite standard we failed to meet, Christ met, and the price we could not pay, He paid in full. What we could not do ourselves, He graciously did for us. Yet His grace does not end there. We do not start with grace and finish with works. Neither does holiness result from us doing our thing and God doing His. It comes from God graciously working in us. Paul put it this way to the Ephesians:

> For by grace have you been saved through faith; and that not of yourselves, it is the gift of God; not as a result of works, that no one should boast. For we are His workmanship, created in Christ Jesus for good works, which God prepared beforehand, that we would walk in them (2:8-10).

Or, as Paul said elsewhere:

> . . . work out your salvation with fear and trembling; for it is God who is at work in you both to will and work for His good pleasure (Phil. 2:12b-13).

As God works *in* us, we *work out* our sanctification with reverential awe. We could not work out our sanctification if it were not for God working in us. His work in us is what makes it possible for us to walk in the good works He prepared beforehand. From start to finish, our salvation is all of grace.

When we earlier called on Promise Keepers to "raise the standard," we did not mean that Promise Keepers (the movement) somehow was to set the standard on its own or to encourage promise keepers (the men involved) to set their own standards since, as we already have seen, there is but one infinite standard: God in Christ as revealed in Scripture. Nor did we mean that Promise Keepers or promise keepers need to do more to measure up to that infinite standard since, as we also have seen, we have not measured up because we cannot do so in ourselves.

The Challenge Ahead

What did we mean by calling on Promise Keepers to raise the standard? Simply this: To recognize that Christ is the only standard. Hence, Promise Keepers needs to "raise the standard" by *exalting the person and work of Christ*. Nothing less will do. Were Promise Keepers to exalt Christ in this way, it would meet the challenge set before it. In this book, we have seen that the challenge indeed is great. We have called attention to several concerns related to the movement and its message. Yet the concerns expressed here, if received with the spirit with which they have been offered, become positive challenges. In particular, we call upon Promise Keepers and promise keepers alike to:

• Recover and proclaim the true gospel of justification by grace alone through faith alone on account of Christ alone;

• Understand the meaning of true, biblical masculinity by calling men to lead, not to follow, their wives and children in every way under God and according to His Word, and by challenging men to relate to one another as men;

• Turn from the covenant of works and cling to the covenant of grace as the only means of relating to God and embrace the covenantal institutions of the family, the church, and the civil order as the only such institutions ordained by God;

• Recognize where psychology clashes with Scripture and remain faithful to the true biblical message, even when that means rejecting psychology as a false gospel;

• Demonstrate true integrity by confessing a lack of discretion in promoting *The Masculine Journey* and by repudiating the book publicly;

- Focus on truth, not technique, in establishing its future goals, conferences, and studies, all the while remaining faithful in its exposition of the Word of God;

- Avoid unbiblical oaths and vows and warn men that it is better not to vow than to vow and not pay;

- Worship God in spirit and truth only as He has prescribed in His Word of truth and cling to that Word of truth as the all-sufficient and self-sufficient standard for everything that is to be believed and done;

- Promote honesty and intimacy in marriage by teaching men to seek forgiveness from their wives for sins committed against their wives, not using small groups as a substitute for the honesty and intimacy that is to characterize the marital relationship;

- Teach that purity is not merely a matter of outward conduct but of inward thoughts and desires and ensure that what is taught is consistent across the board and down the line;

- Exhort men to become the husbands and fathers that God has called them to be, even when that may be at odds with the desires of their wives and children;

- Support the local church in word and deed by doing nothing to rival it as the primary institution for the proclamation of the Word and the administration of the ordinances, by encouraging small groups to form only under the oversight of the local church, and by retracting the covenant of confidentiality as an unbiblical vow;

- Promote true reconciliation and unity in the church, which can only be built upon the rock solid foundation of

the truth of the gospel and cease from promoting the unbiblical concept of reparational reconciliation; and,

• View the vocational calling of men as one important
way men bear witness for Christ by teaching the priesthood
of all believers.

True Integrity on the Line

Earlier, we referred to the situation when Paul had to
confront Peter at Antioch. Peter was a great man, but like
all of us, he had his failings. Paul there rebuked him for the
sin of hypocrisy (Gal. 2:13). But our respect for Peter grows
when we realize that he *received* this rebuke from a brother
as a brother. The problem had been over the relationship of
Jews and Gentiles within the Christian church, and after
receiving Paul's rebuke, Peter actually went on to articulate
and defend Paul's position at the Jerusalem council. He was
a great man indeed—a man of true integrity.

In our fallen world, perfection is not the *sine qua non* of
a genuine and sincere faith. David fell into grievous sin and
yet he was a true saint. But when the Scriptures are pointedly brought to bear on a problem, we must expect those
who love the Word of God to receive it and submit to it.
Such was David's reaction. When David was rebuked by
Nathan, he received it humbly and repented of his grievous
sin. Another man of true integrity.

In bringing our concerns to the Promise Keepers, we
have done so in the hope that the organization will similarly
receive what we have said, and compare it against the Scriptures. We have no desire to write as trouble-makers within
the body of Christ. God hates six things, and seven are an
abomination to Him—including the sin of stirring up dis-
cord among brethren (Prov. 6:16-19). We have no desire to
fall into this sin, and we have no desire to encourage it in
others.

Nevertheless, it is natural that a book like this would create some controversy. We recognize this as a regrettable necessity, but it was most certainly not our goal. As we discuss these issues further, we want our demeanor to continue to be that of *brothers,* not as unreasonable and impossible-to-please-heresy-buster-types. We have sought to present our concerns fairly, and with the genuine desire that Promise Keepers would respond in the same fashion. We can say in all honesty that if the positions were reversed, we would be pleased to be treated the way we have sought to treat Promise Keepers. We have sought to apply the teaching of the Lord throughout. We have done as we would be willing to have done to us.

Further, we have remembered that our Lord has forbidden us to judge with a double standard. "Judge not, that you be not judged. For with what judgment you judge, you will be judged; and with the measure you use, it will be measured back to you" (Matt. 7:1-2). Christ is not prohibiting discernment and evaluation, because in verse 15 of the same chapter, He commands His followers to be on the lookout for false teachers. What He insists upon in the first two verses is that we apply the same standard to ourselves that we apply to others. We believe that teachers are to be held to a stricter standard (Jas. 3:1), and this includes *us* as well as the Promise Keepers. This means that we should be willing to do anything we have asked Promise Keepers to do. For example, we have called upon Promise Keepers to demonstrate true integrity by repudiating its erroneous teaching and the erroneous teachings of others, something it has refused to do so far. But the same standard applies to us as well. If anything we have written here is shown to be in error, we will not pretend that it did not happen. We will publicly retract the error and apologize for having made it.

Our conviction is that a great deal depends upon how Promise Keepers responds to the biblical challenge we have offered. E. Glenn Wagner, Vice President of Ministry Advancement for Promise Keepers, has correctly observed that certainly there "are occasions that call for confrontation and rebuke, but the end result should be restoration and growth, not destruction."† This is one such occasion.

Now it is up to Promise Keepers to demonstrate true integrity by receiving what we have said and acting upon it. If Promise Keepers receives the challenge we have offered, repents of its failures, and brings forth the fruit fitting repentance, then "restoration and growth" will follow. But if Promise Keepers hardens its position, and continues to defend the indefensible, then we, along with all Christians concerned for the authority of Scripture and the gospel of Christ would have no choice but to move from being concerned, to opposing the movement and its message outright.

Men of Promise

As we have said, Promise Keepers needs to raise the standard by exalting the person and work of Christ. Officially, it does. Its statement of belief claims that "Promise Keepers adheres to the foundational truths of historic Christianity which center on the person and work of Jesus Christ."[1] Would that Promise Keepers did what it says by truly raising the standard—by truly exalting the person and work of Christ!

And therein lies the problem. In the name of centering on Christ, Promise Keepers too often has centered on man. It has called on men to become transformed by making promises, instead of calling on them to run to Christ in whom all the promises of God find their "yes" and "amen." It has called men to become promise keepers, forgetting that there has been, and is only one Promise Keeper.

Shocking as it may seem, our fundamental problem is that we all are promise breakers, from the well-dressed professional in the pew beside his wife and children, to the wino in the gutter who split from home ten years ago. We have all said one thing and done another. We have all intended to change but have remained the same.

The answer does not lie within. It lies without. The hope is not in here, but out there. If we understand that hope, if we have found the answer, we must proclaim it at the top of our lungs. We are not saved by our promise keeping. We are saved by Him and His promise keeping alone.

We need to turn from self and turn to Him. We need to get beyond ourselves—*beyond promises*—clinging to Him and His unbroken promises alone, trusting that by His grace, He will perfect the good work He began in us. We are not promise keepers. We are men of promise—men who rely not on our own promises, but on the *only* Promise Keeper who ever lived: the One who paid the price for each of our broken promises and kept all of His promises for us.

He is faithful and true. What He has promised, He will do. He is our Promise Keeper, and we are His men of promise.

---

† *TAPSB*, p. 14.

David G. Hagopian

David G. Hagopian (B.A., history, University of California, Irvine; J.D., University of Southern California) is currently a business litigator in the California office of the international law firm of Dorsey & Whitney and is a member of the California State Bar, the Orange County Bar Association, the Christian Legal Society, and the Federalist Society for Law and Public Policy.

In addition to pursuing his legal career, Mr. Hagopian also edited and coauthored the book, *Back to Basics: Rediscovering the richness of the Reformed Faith* (Presbyterian & Reformed, 1996) and served as a senior editor of, and contributing author to, *Antithesis: A Review of Contemporary Christian Thought and Culture.*

Mr. Hagopian lives in southern California with his wife, Jamie, and his three children, Brandon, Kirstin, and Anallyce.

Douglas J. Wilson

Douglas J. Wilson (B.A., classical studies; M.A., philosophy, University of Idaho) is pastor of Community Evangelical Fellowship in Moscow, Idaho and a Fellow of Philosophy at New St. Andrews College.

He also serves as the editor of *Credenda/Agenda* magazine and has written two books on marriage and child-rearing: *Reforming Marriage* (Canon Press, 1995) and *Standing on the Promises* (Canon, forthcoming 1996). He has written other books including *Recovering the Lost Tools of Learning* (Crossway Books), *Introductory Logic* (Canon Press) *Latin Grammar* (Canon Press), and *Persuasions* (Canon Press). He contributed to *Back to Basics* and has also contributed articles to publications such as *World, Table Talk, Antithesis, Reformation and Revival Journal,* and *Practical Homeschooling.*

He lives in Idaho with his wife, Nancy, and his three children, Bekah, Nathan, and Rachel.